MICKEY ROURKE

MICKEY ROURKE

An Illustrated Biography

BART MILLS

Sidgwick & Jackson Limited
LONDON

First published in Great Britain in 1988 by Sidgwick & Jackson Limited

ISBN 0-283-99520-3

Designed by Oliver Hickey

Typeset by Rowland Phototypesetting Limited,
Bury St Edmunds, Suffolk

Printed by
Butler and Tanner Limited,
Frome, Somerset

for Sidgwick & Jackson Limited
1 Tavistock Chambers, Bloomsbury Way
London WC1A 2SG

CONTENTS

ONE

Mickey Rourke hasn't shaved in two or three days. His hair looks like it was combed by a shovel. His clothes probably came from the bottom of the hamper.

He doesn't have a perfect complexion. His face lacks the geometrically precise lines and shadows that make stills photographers bring out their back lights. His body is many workouts shy of the firmness required to wear a bandolier on a bare chest.

Rourke's voice is high-pitched and soft, almost feathery. His diction is uncultured and cluttered with casual profanity and imprecise inner-city catchphrases. Sometimes he gets

tongue-tied and relies on looks and shrugs to communicate.

But he smiles. When Rourke smiles, offering his feelings openly and his allegiance fully, you see why he's become such an essential, irreplaceable actor. Directors ask for Rourke when they need a man to display damaged goods. They want him to play the desperation of romance in extremis.

Rourke's characters beg for redemption while they build a wall around themselves. They want to drag you down into the dirt to cleanse your soul. Whether his characters are victims or victimizers, they remain fully sympathetic. They're bad boys who grew up without maturing, leaving intact their capacity to be hurt.

In a fight, a Rourke character battles without quarter, like a kid with no sense of the permanence of some kinds of damage. In a bedroom, in the actual steam and stink of sexual embrace, Rourke on screen plays the scene as if it were the last. Rourke the lover is all there.

And that's why he is so often costumed and made up to look as though he went without sleep and showers to make more than his quota of love. Rourke has become *the* ladies' man of eighties movies. In other eras suavity, spit-curls or a robust manner may have been deemed attractive. Today's most believable screen lovers are impulsive seize-the-moment types, and Rourke is the archetype.

Without any planning on his part, his look and attitudes mesh exactly with his times. He says, 'I had trouble with the sixties and seventies. I'm fifties- and eighties-oriented. Those are times I can get into. They're not peace and love, huggy-kissy times. No freak-out stuff. The fifties and the eighties are cool.

In Alan Parker's Angel Heart Rourke played a private detective sent on a missing-person search by the Devil himself.

'I caught the tail end of the fifties. I remember looking at guys and thinking, those guys are cool, those guys with the tattoos. For me, the sixties were a nightmare, and the seventies I don't remember.'

Since his arrival in 1982 in *Diner* as the prankster who wins the rich girl's heart, Rourke has built a list of credits that have made him the envy of other actors and the despair of the studios. So many other actors say they would like to plan their careers without an eye on the main chance. Rourke actually does appear to choose roles because they will be artistically fulfilling and because he feels an affinity towards the director.

The result has been a series of films that demand to be taken seriously yet have little chance of making big money for their backers. Rourke 'blew his chance' of bankability which his *Diner* costars grabbed – Steve Guttenberg with *Police Academy* and Kevin Bacon with *Footloose*. Instead of fitting himself into established methods of character portrayal, he

appeared in dangerous variations on Hollywood genres. Everyone else wanted to be like Gregory Peck. Rourke wanted to be like Marlon Brando.

He consciously sought a reputation for eccentricity and made no secret of his contempt for the studios' A-list directors. He preferred to work with outcasts like Michael Cimino or directors from other countries, like Alan Parker.

For instance, he made *The Pope of Greenwich Village* (1984) because it offered a chance to duet with another actor's actor, Eric Roberts. Never mind that Rourke's and Roberts' interpretations of two small-time cousins and hustlers broke so many of Hollywood's caper-movie conventions that the mass audience was scared off.

In 1985, Rourke did *Year of the Dragon* for Cimino, knowing that Cimino had become a pariah after *Heaven's Gate*. In part, Rourke took the role of the driven, almost psychotic policeman because Cimino had befriended the then-unknown Rourke during the making of *Heaven's Gate*. It was Rourke who took the

heat for the Press' outrage at Cimino's daring to make another movie.

Rourke knowingly walked into the line of fire again in 1986, when he made *Angel Heart* for Alan Parker. When the film came out in 1987, and all too many critics reviewed his chin stubble instead of his acting, Rourke again found himself the victim of his own adventurousness.

Again and again, Rourke has gone out of his way to be misunderstood and maligned, knowing he's living in an era of safe choices and easy millions. But Rourke isn't picking fights. Doing what he feels he must, he gets swatted time after time. Every time, he's just as surprised as the time before. He's like a kid who won't learn that fire is hot.

So Rourke is not a happy man. He feels more and more isolated with every rebuff and self-inflicted wound. Talk to him, and he'll pour out a stream of anger and disappointment. Then look at the film he does next, and it's just as off-centre, just as challenging as the last one.

Making *Barfly* in Los Angeles in 1987,

In Year of the Dragon *Rourke played a New York police captain obsessed with nicking a Chinatown druglord played by John Lone.*

Rourke played a scene one day in which he toasted the dedicated drinkers who shared space at his favourite bar. 'To all my friends,' Rourke's character said. 'To all my friends.'

Rourke is a man who likes to be surrounded by friends, because he knows that just outside the campfire's glow many enemies lurk. Wherever you see Rourke, on a set or between jobs, he keeps his friends near.

When he's working, he brings his own caravan, a silver Airstream trailer he affectionately calls 'the Fish'. He stocks the Fish with people he met last week and people he's known for years. Relentlessly social, always in need of a sounding board, Rourke acquires people with his generosity and keeps them through his loyalty. He gives them jobs, they give him their ears.

Rourke and his buddies travel together, taking a long holiday from responsibility and permanence. Rourke is a married man, but he prefers living in hotel rooms. He kept a room at the Mayflower Hotel in New York for years

11

In Prayer for the Dying *Rourke played an IRA cemetery filler who tries to lay down the gun after one last murder.*

while his wife Debra Feuer preferred their house in Los Angeles. Even when he's in Los Angeles, Rourke likes to spend time at an apartment which he calls his office but which looks more like a clubhouse.

Among his pals, none of whom are his peers in the business, Rourke can smile and laugh and shoot the shit without fear of contradiction. They provide a warm and safe harbour away from the business, from which he feels increasingly alienated.

Rourke is a man to nurse grudges. He has his enemies, and they know who they are. They are certain members of the Press, writers whose comments on Michael Cimino stopped short of total adulation. Rourke doesn't mind most criticism of himself, but he feels enraged when people he trusts are treated badly.

More recently, Rourke has been thrown into a depression by his bad experience making *Prayer for the Dying* in England in 1986. He is scathing on the subject of Samuel Goldwyn Jr, whose American company, The Goldwyn Co., partially backed the film, a drama set in London against the background of the troubles in Northern Ireland.

Rourke says he was rendered almost unfit for further work by his experience working with Goldwyn. But the actor is a battler. In choosing next to make *Barfly*, Rourke took on another close-to-the-edge character, but one whose travails resonate with his own. Like Rourke, the character is an ex-boxer who is forced to keep on fighting long after he hangs up the gloves. And like Rourke, the character is an artist who prefers not to get sucked into safe and sensible ways of expressing his vision.

So Rourke brought himself back through work — though not so much through work as through defiant self-expression. Rourke believes in 'moments'. As an actor, his task is to create the reality of each moment in the audience's mind. In his life, too, Rourke responds to 'moments', making long-range decisions on the spur of the moment, responding to an inner urge that seems to be new every minute but is remarkably consistent.

This has always been the pattern of Rourke's life. From the start, he has lived in the moment, not for the long run. He stopped boxing, for instance, because excelling in the ring would have required long hours of uninteresting preparation. He gravitated towards acting because every step and every syllable offer chances for variation and experimentation. He spent years in acting class in New York City before venturing out on the street to embark on a career because he genuinely enjoyed the creativeness of acting 'exercises'.

Rourke might be happier today earning nothing in acting class than he is earning millions above the title. He certainly enjoys the money his acting success brings him, but he uses it the same way he would use lesser sums: to build and stock playrooms for himself and his circle. He is not a snappy dresser or a frequenter of pretentious eateries. T-shirts and cords, bars and rock clubs are more his style.

Working freely 'in the moment' is his life, and he hates the commercial forces that conspire to limit that freedom. He decidedly does not want to harness these forces for his own ends, as some actors have succeeded in doing. He wants to fight them or evade them but never to join them.

So this most combative of actors may wind up with whatever is the performer's equivalent of cauliflower ears. But as he fights, he will retain the interest of those who love dangerous, high-wire acting.

TWO

Rourke wouldn't be as honest playing low-lifes today if he hadn't been raised to be one. He had a storybook childhood in the tradition of *Oliver Twist* and *Lord of the Flies*. From his crowded, impoverished background, he learned distrust, disrespect, inconstancy, prevarication, self-indulgence, self-laceration – all the qualities you forget when he smiles.

Growing up unhappy in a bad neighbourhood in Miami, Rourke became a master at getting into trouble and getting out again. He was his own worst enemy, though his friends ran him a close second. His home was a battlefield where Mickey and his brother Joey were always outnumbered by their five stepbrothers and outgunned by their stepfather, a policeman.

It was an upbringing likely to produce an antisocial fighter, and it did. Less probably, his upbringing also fostered Rourke's capacity for dreamy withdrawal. In his life, Rourke has always been sustained by his combativeness; in his work, on the other hand, he has needed the ability to imagine himself into other lives. When he was fighting his teachers by ostentatiously not paying attention, he was creating the fantasies an actor can spend his whole career feeding off. Everybody is moulded by the past, Rourke believes. You can advance, but the past will always be with you.

Rourke was born in the small city of Schenectady in upstate New York in September, 1954. He was christened Philip Andre Rourke, the same name as his father. His Irish ancestry assured the boy the nickname Mickey. Rourke senior worked as a caretaker at a golf club and spent his off hours lifting weights.

Rourke's mother and father were continually at loggerheads, often driving Rourke downstairs to his grandmother's apartment. There the boy could escape his parents' bickering by watching TV and eating the goodies grandma would bake for him.

When he was seven, his parents divorced. Mrs Rourke and her mother and her three children moved to Miami. As Rourke later remembered the separation, it was painful and dramatic. His mother and grandmother told him they were taking him on a trip. They said they would buy him a horse. Before they left, his father came into his room and told him the truth. The boy raged against the split, vowing not to go.

Mickey and his brother Joey grew up unhappily in Miami, stuffed into one bedroom with five step-brothers. Joey later survived cancer.

13

But they did take Rourke away, and the boy never reconciled himself to his fate. Although Rourke wasn't in touch with his father from the time of their separation until nearly twenty years later, after the younger man had committed himself to becoming an actor, he always carried a picture of his well-muscled dad. Although his Miami stepfather asked Rourke to call him 'Dad', the boy never would. Rourke's brother Joey did, and Mickey remembered feeling betrayed.

Mrs Rourke's remarriage to the Miami policeman, a widower, came just a year after the family had resettled in Miami. They were living in the back of a launderette that Mrs Rourke had opened in Liberty City, a rough, mostly black area of Miami. A few years after Rourke left Miami there was a riot in the district in which eighteen people were killed.

Along with the hated stepfather, five hated stepbrothers moved in, and all five crammed in with Mickey and Joey. A three-decker bunk bed ensured unpleasantly close quarters in the bedroom. When Rourke fell out of his top rack, the landings weren't soft, and he still hasn't forgiven his stepbrothers for their derision. What was he doing living with these people? he wondered.

'There's not much you can do at that age. You either click on or you click off. And I clicked off for years. When you're a kid, you wake up in the morning or try to go to sleep at night and you say, "Why me? Why is this happening to me?" Now I've got to look at it and, honestly, all I can say is I got two legs and two arms and a brother who's healthy, a sister, my mother is alive. I look at it that way now. But then, it was a nightmare.'

Home was uncongenial, and so was school. Rourke recollected promising his father just before they parted that he would get back at everybody and everything by not learning anything at school. It was one promise he kept. He just sat at the back of the class taking up space. He didn't want to take part, and more often than not he just put his head down on the table.

Put in classes for slow learners, he scraped through by cheating. 'I got my grandfather to do my homework for me but he did it all wrong. Anyway, he wrote like a carpenter and when I took the papers in, the teachers knew I hadn't done them.'

At an early age Rourke became an accomplished liar. 'If you grow up in harmony, let's call it, you don't have to lie. But if you live in disharmony, then you have to lie and lie good. When I was a young kid, I would start talking to friends, and I'd make shit up that would amaze myself. I couldn't tell the truth if you hit me over the fucking head with it. I'd be lying and really believing it. I noticed a lot of other guys doing it, too. When you're so fucked up, confused and unhappy, you have to make shit up to feel good. I think a certain amount of that probably helps me say other people's lines with conviction. That was the difference between me and my brother Joe. I would rather lie than get hit. My brother Joe would never lie, no matter what.'

When Rourke was fifteen, the family moved to Miami Beach, a few miles away and a few notches higher on the socio-economic scale. Again, Rourke's wishes weren't taken into account. He loved being in Liberty City and hanging out with the black kids there, he said later.

Rourke rebelled, as he has done in many circumstances, by pretending he was somewhere else. He came into Miami Beach dressed like a soul brother from the ghetto: 'My brother and I were used to wearing pointed black shoes, white socks, different-coloured T-shirts. Everyone in Miami was colour-coordinated. They called us Hooples, until my brother hit one of them with a baseball bat. To them, we were like the Jesse James gang. But we weren't really bad – we were different . . . Plus, the level of [schoolwork] there – the people seemed smarter.'

Home and school had failed Rourke, so he lived for sports. Although he had potential as a baseball player and boxer, he threw away his opportunities at an early age by refusing to accept his coaches' discipline. After provoking the coach, he was thrown off his high school baseball team just before a visit by scouts from the professional leagues.

As for boxing, Rourke takes the sport far more seriously now than he did as a boy. Starting when he was fourteen, he trained for four years at Miami's Fifth St Gym. For a while, all his ambitions were wrapped up in boxing. He fought and won four bouts in the Police Athletic League, the standard starting point for American fighters.

He loved boxing because it was a chance to prove himself one-on-one. But he progressed no further because he wasn't disciplined. He

In Nicolas Roeg's Eureka Rourke played the villain's hatchetman, a soft-spoken yes-man adept at dinner party repartee, arson and murder.

would lie to his trainer about putting in his miles of roadwork. Today, echoing Brando's line from *On the Waterfront*, Rourke believes that he coulda been a contender. But he'll never know how far he could have gone. 'When I was boxing back in Miami, I didn't have my head on right. I didn't do the road work. I didn't practise the things I was told to. I quit boxing basically because I wasn't willing to go the distance.'

A boxing background came in handy when Rourke became an actor. 'There's a physicalness that I'm very comfortable with. Any scene with action in it comes natural to me, from being an athlete. But as much time as I spent being an athlete, I spent chain-smoking cigars in a coffee shop.'

In the coffee shops and in the streets, Rourke and his pals adopted a Little Havana lifestyle. Clothes made the man. Every time he had $100 in his pocket, he would go and have another pair of platform shoes made in egregious colours like turquoise. Tight pants, cut-off shirts and long blow-dried hair completed the look.

'I didn't know why I was dressed that way back in Miami. I just liked the dudes I was hanging with because they were loose, man; they weren't uptight.' This aimless group had 'nothing on our minds but a good fucking time, a good fucking girl. During the day, we'd go down to 48th St Beach. We used to wear little tiny bathing suits, lay out in the sun, take half a dozen Seconals. We were big on downers back then. Everybody would talk in slow motion. Everybody would be checking themselves out when they spoke. You never heard so much lying and bragging. Everybody was into being cool, being tough, getting down and getting high.

'I'm totally anti-drugs. I had my fling, but it wasn't for that long. All those legends, a lot of them aren't around now. A lot of them are dead.'

In those days, Rourke worked when he had to, and no more often. In a typically half-hearted move, he took a job as an electrician — for one day. 'This guy showed me how to work some machine that bent pipes, but I couldn't figure out how it worked, so I stared at the machine all day. Plus, I have this thing about getting shocks.'

For a time, he was an usher in a movie theatre. He got in a fight with another usher, 'who conked me over the head with a flashlight, and I got fired.'

He was and he remains an attitude case. 'I didn't like my foreman when I was in construction. I didn't like the guys around the warehouse when I worked in the warehouse. I didn't like punching the clock when I had to punch a clock. I didn't even like the customers when I laid linoleum. I'm a free man, Jack; I can do what I want to do when I want to do it. I did it when I wasn't getting paid and I do it now.'

One of his dead-end jobs did lead to something. Miami Beach is full of hotels. Every hotel has a pool, and every pool has pool boys. Rourke used to get up before school and lay out the mats by the pools. A friend from his pool boy days later became involved with theatre at a local community college. For some reason, the friend called Rourke to play the part of Green Eyes in Jean Genet's *Death Watch*.

'I went down there and did this Genet thing with him, a showcase, about a black guy and a white guy on death row. I really liked it. I don't think I was very good, you know, in that first thing. But it was like, "Hey, this is a great feeling. Whatever this is, this is neat."' Rourke repeated the role at another local theatre and concluded that it was the first worthwhile thing he had done in three or four years.

It wasn't cool to admit this to the guys popping downers at the beach. Rourke was living with five other lowlifes in a Miami motel called the Wild West, and he was beginning to realize that he couldn't keep on living this way indefinitely.

'You can only get by with the kind of shit I was into for so long. The whole young macho trip. Fighting, having big balls. You can't survive that way in this day and age. And I knew that. I was nineteen. I didn't want to be a professional bad-ass.'

One day, lying on the beach, he and a pal were discussing larceny. The pal was called Stoney Curtis because he was dark and handsome like Tony Curtis and he liked to get high. 'He was just out of jail and we were talking about some things we were maybe gonna do. But then I said, "No, man, I'm gonna be an actor. I'm gonna go to New York."'

THREE

Rourke tells a pathetic yet typical story about his arrival in New York in 1975. He was a kid from deepest Florida with only the vaguest of ambitions, the thinnest of wardrobes, the oddest of misconceptions.

'I was totally uneducated about New York. Everybody told me before I left, "Whatever you do, don't trust any black cab drivers." They said, "Don't get in a cab with a black driver, cause he's gonna rip you off!"'

'So I got off a plane in New York and all these regular, innocent-looking black guys are coming up to me: "Hey, you need a cab?" And I'm saying, "No, man, I don't need no fuckin' cab." This is how fucking backward I was. Standing there and waiting, like, hours for a white driver. See what I mean? I was a fucking yo-yo.'

Yo-yo or no, Rourke knew where he wanted to go – to the Actors Studio, the famed acting centre where he had heard Steve McQueen once studied. So when he finally found a cab he went directly to the school, carrying his suitcases. Accustomed to oddities walking in off the street, the people there treated him politely.

They eventually steered him in the direction of the sort of accommodation he could afford – a flophouse that catered to people on state assistance. The boy from Miami, hip as he thought he was, thought he was at the This Way to Hell Hotel. Every night, he took to bed with him the club the Miami gang had given him to protect himself from all those New York weirdos out of *Midnight Cowboy*.

For a while, Rourke was as lost in Manhattan as Jon Voight's character had been. Rourke had promised himself that he would give that acting stuff five years. But at first he found himself spending all his energy just figuring out how to survive.

Looking back now, he says he would give anything to be able to go back to that time. He'd love to be so much in awe of something again. At the time, though, it was a day-to-day struggle. He recalls fighting off the advances of men he only belatedly understood to be homosexual. He stubbornly continued dressing for the Miami sunshine in his platform shoes and patterned pants. He took jobs that he proved incompetent at. He spent a lot of time at the telegraph office waiting for the small sum his grandmother sent him monthly. When he had to, he lived on shoplifted candy bars. He didn't actually do much about becoming an actor.

The jobs Rourke got were mostly entry-level positions for a lifetime of going nowhere. He parked cars for a while, but his reversing was too poor to consider a career in garage management. He functioned as an assistant to a guard dog trainer. He was a Good Humour man, driving a neighbourhood ice cream van. He was an attendant at a rifle range. He was a towel boy in massage parlours. He moved furniture in a warehouse where McQueen, Lee Marvin and Gene Hackman had sweated before him.

For a time, he was a pretzel and chestnut vendor. He and a pal would walk down to Greenwich Village to get the pretzel carts and then they'd push them uptown to Central Park. They'd stop and sell when they could, but they'd usually be chased away by the vendors who had prior claim on the locations. Finally they would find a corner nobody had claimed. Then, at night, they would push the carts all the way back.

For part of the time when Rourke was first

in New York, he had the company of a buddy from Miami, known as Little Eddie. Eddie roomed with Rourke at the Marlton Hotel on West Eighth St, and he was not a good influence. Rourke would do anything for his pal, including minimizing Eddie's shortness by walking in the gutter when a girl passed by them on the pavement. Eddie's inclinations were larcenous, and Rourke came close to involvements he might have later regretted.

Another influence at the Marlton was more positive: Carl Montgomery, the night manager. A stage buff, Carl showed Rourke his collection of theatre programmes and clippings about the stars. He took Rourke to his first Broadway show. He helped him change his look from faded Havana glitz to the scruffy Manhattan style he still favours today.

Eventually, Rourke remembered why he was in New York, and he wandered back to the Actors Studio. With its restricted membership and emphasis on a particular technique, 'the Method', the Actors Studio itself is more of a lab for professionals. Attached to it are various teachers and coaches who each have their own clientele of aspiring actors. One of them is Sandra Seacat.

Rourke believes that Sandra Seacat is the greatest acting coach in the world, the best since Stanislavski, the famed Russian originator of Method acting. 'She saw something in me worthy of her time and attention. It was the first real guidance I'd had. Without her guidance, I wouldn't have continued with acting. She made everything click.

'Acting wasn't a normal sort of thing to do. I used to see these people in class and I didn't know what the fuck they were doing. I was supposed to be learning acting and the teachers were asking me to bring in pots and pans? Now I'd know what they were trying to do, but then I didn't. It took me a couple of years.'

At first, Rourke attended Seacat's classes without participating. It was like his school days in Miami, when the sight of an authority figure turned him cataleptic. He was terrified of revealing anything about himself.

'I'm a very slow learner. I was a late bloomer when it came to growing up. It took me quite a few years to get my stuff together because I had no great drive to be an actor. There's a large part of me that doesn't want to open up. As an actor, you have to open up. I spent my whole life keeping things to myself,

so all of a sudden I'm going to let it all out?'

Eventually, Seacat broke through his defences. On one particular day, Rourke was so angry that other students were doing improvizations without difficulty that he opened up. Seacat asked him to get up in front and shine his shoes. Because she told him to do some physical action, he forgot about the rest of the class. Then she asked him to lace up his baseball cleats. Suddenly Rourke broke down, remembering the special place in his life baseball used to hold. Breaking down like that was like going through a barrier for Rourke. For the first time in years he let the emotion come out.

To this day, Seacat remains one of the gods in Rourke's small pantheon. Rourke blossomed, channelling what was holding him back into something creative and challenging. He put in a lot of time watching actors on the screen, moving beyond his earlier taste for McQueen, Bronson and Eastwood. He decided he wanted to make uncompromising movies with good characters.

'I had no great passion to be an actor until relatively late. Now you see these guys twenty, twenty-one, twenty-two, doing all these movies. When I was their age I couldn't have done that, and I respect what they can do. I'm also glad that I did what I was doing then, because it lends itself to what I'm doing now. I rely on those experiences when I have to do moments in front of the camera. Being a normal person at one time is something I can use now.'

Rourke's success in acting class began looking like another dead end, and Rourke's reluctance to compromise kept him from progressing. He was cast in several off-off-Broadway productions but played few roles before audiences because he would usually quarrel with his directors. According to Seacat, Rourke would never stick with these productions. If they weren't going the way he wanted them to, he would leave.

It was at Seacat's urging that at this point in his life Rourke reestablished his relationship with his father. He was preparing his audition piece for the Actors Studio itself, a scene from *Cat on a Hot Tin Roof* between Brick and Big Daddy. Seacat thought Rourke could resolve problems he was having with the scene if he resolved similar problems in his own life.

So Rourke took the bus up to Schnectady

guys twice my age who had been at the Studio for years and had never gotten any recognition. I'm not talking about non-talented guys. Then I'd go to the movies and see twenty-year-old kids making a quarter of a million bucks. Why were those talented people in the little room on 44th St and the other guys out there getting rich? I just couldn't understand it.

'You could work and work in class, do pure work and be an artist. That's all fine and dandy, you know, but, like, who really cares, who really fucking cares? I'm glad I had that experience, but I decided I had to make my own rules.'

The way the Actors Studio was run turned out to be uncongenial to Rourke's thin-skinned sensibilities. 'I saw all the power trips people were on.' Specifically, he couldn't take criticism from the head of the Studio, the ageing actors' guru, Lee Strasberg. In Rourke's eyes, Strasberg's coaching amounted to carping. When Strasberg nailed him once, Rourke walked out for good.

Still studying with Seacat, Rourke was cast in her showcase production of Arthur Miller's *A View from the Bridge*. Rourke's portrayal of Eddie, the driven, murderous protagonist (played by Raf Vallone in the 1962 film) drew praise from Miller himself. For the first time, the idea of seeking film and television work in Hollywood was presented to Rourke. But he preferred to stay in New York, where he was comfortably settled as king of the acting classes.

Seacat knew when it was time to push Rourke out of the nest. In 1978, 'She let me have it. We were standing on Eighth Avenue in the middle of the night in the pouring rain, and she was screaming at me, "What are you turning into?" She was yelling, "Do you want to take classes for the rest of your life? Do something! Get out there! Work!"'

and saw his father for the first time in seventeen years. It was a cordial but somewhat uninvolving reunion from Rourke's point of view, preoccupied as he was with playing Brick, not himself. The young actor-to-be noticed with disappointment that his father's muscles had gone to flab. He accepted $50, bussed back to New York and passed his audition. Although Rourke corresponded with his father in the years after their meeting, he never saw him again.

In the Actors Studio, Rourke began to come into his own. He supported Ron Leibman in a closed-doors production of *Richard III*. The actor he felt closest to at the Studio was Christopher Walken, who was yet to make *The Deer Hunter*.

But as soon as he realized that acting could be a career, his disillusionment began. 'I saw

FOUR

Rourke recalls most of his life in a series of dramatic bursts, but his recollections of his first days in Los Angeles are sketchy. He does tell a story about living in a flophouse and walking up and down Sunset Boulevard, looking for any kind of job and finally finding one parking cars at a restaurant.

He had borrowed money to get to the Coast, but on this migration he didn't arrive as a complete unknown. He had already been signed by managers Bob LeMond and Lois Zetter, who also managed John Travolta. But managers can only chart a career's direction; they can't get an actor work. For that, Rourke needed an agent.

'Lois introduced me to different agents. One lady couldn't make up her mind for a year whether to take me, and another one told me to go back to New York and forget about it, and then I talked to Bernie [Carneol], and he asked me to come in and do a contemporary and a classical monologue for him. So I did, and when I was finished Bernie just pushed the paper towards me, and I signed, and we been rockin' and rollin' ever since.

'He's a young guy. He started his own agency after being in acting. So we started to click together and he worked around the clock for me.' To start with, Carneol began getting Rourke TV one-shots – bit parts on episodic television.

At this stage of an actor's career, the emphasis is on getting performances on film, no matter how minor the part or modest the production. The tapes of his scenes can then be hawked around the offices of casting directors who can offer more substantial parts.

It was good experience, he still believes. Even dwarfs start small. The first directors Rourke worked with were men he didn't even want to be in the same room with. But Rourke somehow managed to bite his tongue when his idealistic sensibilities were wounded by the frenetic pace of television production and the lowered expectations of those who crank out channel fodder for the American networks.

Rourke was one of those lucky actors whose unique qualities shone out immediately. He quickly graduated from weekly series to feature films and TV movies. He appeared very briefly in Steven Spielberg's *1941* and in *Fade to Black* (1980).

In 1979 he was hired for Michael Cimino's *Heaven's Gate*. 'I was supposed to have been Christopher Walken's partner. The part never developed. I just hung around the set. I stayed twelve weeks.'

His roles were better in TV movies, though he is not proud of having done them and usually avoids mentioning them. As he looks back on them, he was just going through the motions, so he could move on to doing the kind of movies he wanted to do. The three TV movies Rourke made were far from drivel. *City in Fear*, a three-hour production broadcast on ABC in 1980, was a vehicle for David Janssen (who died shortly after it was made). Janssen played a columnist egged into turning a serial killer's crimes into a circulation-builder. Rourke was seventh-billed. *Act of Love*, which also aired in 1980 and was also directed by Jud Taylor, brought Rourke up to third billing. He played a paralysed motorcyclist and Ron Howard was his mercy-killer brother.

Rourke's third TV movie proved he could be a leading man, albeit an unconventional one. *Rape and Marriage: The Rideout Case*, which went out 30 October 1980, was a docudrama about an actual case of marital rape in Oregon in 1978. John Rideout, played

Rourke's first leading part was in a TV movie, Rape and Marriage: The Rideout Case, *in which he played a man prosecuted for raping his wife.*

by Rourke, was the first husband put on trial for sexually assaulting his wife while they were living together. 'There are good performances here by Mickey Rourke and Linda Hamilton,' wrote *Los Angeles Times* critic Howard Rosenberg. 'However, one feels oddly aloof and unconcerned about its characters, who are essentially unsympathetic – especially John, who is weak and a violent wife-abuser.'

At this point in his career, a talented young American actor must choose whether to play for all the marbles. Television can bring comfort, recognition, good money – and also typecasting, job dissatisfaction and early burnout. The movies reward superior actors who resist classification – but there are far fewer parts available. An actor can go broke or go mad waiting for that career-making feature film part.

Describing that point in his life, Rourke recalls being offered half a million dollars to do a miniseries for TV. He was broke at the time and working as a bouncer in a transvestite nightclub on Hollywood Boulevard. His agent advised him to wait, and Rourke waited. But he didn't have to wait long before Larry Kasdan showed him his script for *Body Heat.* 'My role in *Body Heat* wasn't that big. At the time I could have gotten bigger roles. But it was something I could get into, so I took it.'

Kasdan had written hits for George Lucas and Steven Spielberg, and *Body Heat* was his first crack at directing. Rourke's part in the 1981 film was almost a footnote to the main plot, in which William Hurt and Kathleen Turner made steamy love and made themselves stars. Richard Crenna, as Turner's husband, revived his flagging career, and Ted Danson as a friendly prosecutor laid the foundation for later TV stardom in *Cheers.*

Rourke had just two scenes. As he says,

In a two-scene role in Body Heat *Rourke received career-making reviews as an arsonist who advises lawyer William Hurt on how to be a criminal.*

they were written very well, but they were also played very well. They were the first indication that, no matter how high the level, every scene Rourke is in belongs to Rourke.

Rourke is Teddy Lewis, a South Florida arsonist whom Hurt has previously defended successfully. So when the illicit lovers scheme to kill Crenna and immolate his body in a beachfront property called The Breakers, Hurt turns to the torching expert, Rourke.

First we see the firebomb. Then we hear the rock music, by Bob Seger, in such sharp contrast with the rest of the violin-filled score which was inspired by *film noir*. Then we see Rourke, miming to the tune. He's wearing a black T-shirt and jeans, with one pearl earring. This is a proletarian, a mechanic of crime, in contrast to Hurt, the tomcatting defence lawyer who never got his hands dirty before. Rourke knows about crime; Hurt is just a dilettante.

'Are you listening to me, asshole? Because I like you. I got a serious question for you. What the fuck are you doing? This is not shit for you to be messing with.'

Rourke's tough dialogue, delivered in his soft, high voice, immediately established him as an actor drawn to ambiguity. Lines like

those are often heard in action movies, but they're rarely delivered by a sympathetic character. Instead of playing Teddy Lewis as a standard-issue criminal, Rourke turned him into the only character in the movie worth even half a cheer.

He warns Hurt; 'Any time you try a decent crime, you got fifty ways you could fuck up. If you think of twenty-five of 'em, then you're a genius. And you ain't no genius.' Rourke's wise words are just what the audience is thinking. Of course Hurt does the job and of course he doesn't get away with it. As the noose is tightening, Rourke reappears.

He's in jail. He is unshaven, and now his T-shirt is white. He talks even more softly as he gives Hurt the first inkling that his beautiful co-conspirator has been working solo all the time. 'You better watch your step.' Forewarned, Hurt avoids one Turner trap but falls into another. She gets all the money, he goes to prison, and nobody cares what happens to all the secondary characters.

Bits like Teddy Lewis are rarely star-making parts, but something about the kid that played the arsonist made reviewers and film moguls remember his face. The doyenne of American critics, Pauline Kael, wrote in *The New Yorker*: 'The actors in the few minor roles are considerably livelier, and one, Mickey Rourke, who plays Teddy, a professional arsonist, has an awareness of danger that almost makes you feel you're at a real movie. Teddy moves warily, and when he talks about how to set a fire he's hunched over, leaning in close as if he were sharing state secrets with you — he delivers his lines in a diplomatic pouch.'

Even though Rourke knew *Body Heat* was an important breakthrough, he didn't delude himself that he had arrived. The project was a step up in class, but in his view, his work was still compromised. He was a hired hand, doing what he was told to do. He knew he could only do his best work if someone gave him the freedom to do it. Soon afterwards, in *Diner*, Rourke finally got a chance to show what his best work might be.

23

Barry Levinson's Diner *was the film that made Rourke a star. He played a ladies' man who likes to bet on his romantic prowess.*

FIVE

Diner was a flop. It was a film starring nobody with a plot that went nowhere. The company that backed it, MGM, somehow thought it was financing another clone of *Animal House* or *Porky's*, films that had launched the raunchy guys-at-play genre. When MGM saw the final cut of *Diner*, it realized that the film couldn't be sold as that season's gross-out caper. And the studio didn't suspect that the film could be sold as art. *Diner* was tested, shown in a few markets and shelved.

The writer-director, Barry Levinson, finagled a screening for the New York critics. He was hoping for reviews that might persuade MGM that it could release *Diner* profitably in New York and elsewhere. Levinson's hopes were fulfilled. Not only did the journalists adore the idea of a film-maker getting his film in through the back door, they actually loved the film itself. Their response embarrassed MGM into letting the rest of the world see it – though the company's initial fears proved somewhat warranted. *Diner* was a critical hit but never reached a huge audience.

But its second-chance release did at least ensure that everyone's work in it would be seen and appreciated. Levinson went on to become the hot-ticket director of *The Natural* and *Tin Men*, and three of his actors, Steve Guttenberg, Kevin Bacon and Mickey Rourke, became big stars.

Rourke was older than most of his co-stars and had little in common with them. The director's intention – to make a light comedy in a dark style – wasn't clear to him during production. The characters in the film, aimless middle-class boy-men, were strangers to him. It was all make-believe to Rourke. But Rourke grabbed his chance with both hands.

Rourke played Robert 'Boogie' Sheftell, the oldest and most wayward of a group of young men who had been friends in school. Life in the real world wasn't so easy now that the guys were out on their own. The old gang liked to get together after hours at the Fells Point Diner to vent their frustrations, which usually revolved around women.

Daniel Stern was married but he couldn't get his wife to give his record collection the respect it deserved. Guttenberg was about to get married, but he couldn't be sure if his bride would have enough love for the Baltimore Colts football club. Kevin Bacon had lapsed into nihilism and love of the bottle. Paul Reiser was an incurable moocher. Timothy Daly had gotten a girl in trouble but she seemed to think she'd gotten him in trouble. And there was Rourke, in debt up to his eyeballs because of a miscalculation with a bookie.

It's Christmas week, 1959, and the guys at the dance are wondering, 'Hey, have you seen Boogie?' Boogie is the sort of guy who has to be everywhere at once, if only to keep up his image as the guy who always comes through for everybody. He's down in the basement, talking Bacon out of breaking windows. He's out in the corridor, patching things up with Bacon's date.

Boogie is a hairdresser by day, a law student by night, a womanizer around the clock ('Cut and fuck, $2.50,' one of the guys says, admiringly). He's a chancer, confident that his luck and his smile will carry him through. He has gambled $2,000, money he doesn't have, on a supposedly fixed basketball game. But that isn't enough. He tells the guys he has a date with a knockout and asks, 'You wanna bet that she goes for my pecker on our first date?'

This is the set-up for a scene that has gone

(l. to r.) Kevin Baron, Rourke, Daniel Stern and Steve Guttenberg: four of the Baltimore buddies who hang out at the Fells Point Diner.

Rourke with Steve Guttenberg and (seated l. to r.) Daniel Stern, Kevin Baron and Timothy Daly.

down in film history, the scene that made Rourke a star, the pecker-in-the-popcorn scene. In a darkened theatre, that old fifties clunker, *A Summer Place*, is on the big screen. The speakers are churning out dialogue like '. . . as though sex were synonymous with dirt . . .' when Boogie's date finds more in the popcorn box than she'd bargained on.

What makes the scene a classic is Boogie's so-sincere explanation: 'Can I be straight with you . . .?' Rourke shows here how irresistible a naughty boy can be. He admits he's guilty, claims it was an accident, says he couldn't help it, and intrigues her with his detailed excuses.

Compulsively, Boogie digs deeper and deeper holes for himself. He loses the basketball bet and his response is to say to the guys, 'I betcha I can ball Carol Heathrow on the next date.' Meanwhile, he's got his eye on a rich girl on horseback, and in his spare time he's consoling Daniel Stern's neglected wife, played by Ellen Barkin.

In his scenes with Barkin, Rourke walks the thin line between genuine tenderness and complete heartlessness. He wants to use the willing Barkin to win his bet-I-can-ball-her wager, yet he does truly care for her. With Boogie, you can't get one side of him without the other.

Rourke in the popcorn scene from Diner.

In Eureka *Rourke played a buttoned-down bespectacled aide to gangster Joe Pesci. As his career progressed, Rourke proved not to be a coat-and-tie actor at all.*

That's Rourke's gift — to evade classification, to tell the truth while lying, to make you love him while hoping you never get mixed up with somebody as dangerous as him.

Diner is really a series of intertwined anecdotes. A lot of scenes do nothing but build character, and some of them are priceless. Because his character is the outsider in the group, Rourke has most of the best lines. For instance, sitting at the counter of the diner, bridegroom-to-be Steve Guttenberg worries, 'I keep thinking I'm going to be missing out.' Boogie pours sugar straight from the dispenser into his mouth and chases it with Coke. He responds, 'That's what marriage is all about.'

No critic can resist this kind of performance, especially if it's by a new actor in a movie a studio is mishandling. *Rolling Stone* said Rourke 'displays enormous feline charm and speaks in a seductive purr'. *New York Magazine* said, 'The soft-voiced Rourke . . . uses his crinkled eyes and sad smile to make Boogie the most reassuring of con men.' Pauline Kael applauded Rourke: 'The sleaziest and most charismatic figure of the group . . . With luck,

Rourke could become a major actor: he has an edge and magnetism, and a sweet, pure smile that surprises you. He seems to be acting to you, and to no one else.'

Diner was the movie that turned Rourke into the major actor Kael thought he could become, but before it broke he was just another hopeful. He leapt at the chance to spend part of the winter of 1981–2 in the Caribbean working for Nic Roeg playing the third heavy in *Eureka*.

Later, he said he accepted the role because Roeg was a friend and the location was agreeable. But at the time he signed it looked like a good career move to play a Catholic yes-man to Joe Pesci's Jewish gangster.

Rourke appears a third of the way through the film. Gene Hackman has found gold and now, years later, owns a sun-drenched island that Pesci wants to develop. After a short chat on religion, Pesci sends Rourke to Hackman's hideaway to assess his adversary. At the dinner table Hackman's daughter, played by Theresa Russell, performs a feat of mental arithmetic and Rourke says, 'I'm sure that's not your only

Nicolas Roeg, director of Eureka.

talent, Miss McCann.' That's Rourke's one good line in the film. As for getting the girl, Russell is reserved for Rutger Hauer.

Rourke's character is a shy, bespectacled, coat-and-tie kind of guy who makes little impact on anybody. He even tends to push his glasses up the bridge of his nose like Clark Kent. When he leads the gang who blowtorch Hackman, he makes an odd conspirator indeed.

When Roeg's complicated construction finally slipped onto movie screens more than a year later in 1983, Rourke was missed by most reviewers. *The Guardian*'s Tim Pulleine wrote off the film ('Pretension, I'm afraid, finally wins the day') while never mentioning Rourke's performance. *Variety* said, 'Pic reeks of pretentious Art,' and didn't mention Rourke.

In later years, Rourke would inventory his courageous choice of roles like this: '*Body Heat* to *Diner* to *The Pope of Greenwich Village* to *9½ Weeks* to *Year of the Dragon*. They're all different, what do you think?' Maybe the most different of all, *Eureka*, just slipped Rourke's mind.

It was a narrow escape.

SIX

As a follow-up to *Diner*, which Rourke never thought was more than 'a harmless little comedy,' *Rumble Fish* was an intriguing choice. The film, virtually all in black and white, was designed as a mood piece, a sombre meditation on youth culture that might have looked more natural to American audiences if it had been subtitled.

Director Francis Coppola was determined to prove his continued artistic vigour and independence, and by recruiting Rourke to star as 'the Motorcycle Boy' he chose a willing collaborator in experimentation. Coppola had met Rourke while casting the ensemble in *The Outsiders*. There wasn't a part in that film that was right for Rourke, but when the director decided to go ahead with *Rumble Fish* immediately, he called Rourke to his Tulsa location.

Coppola wrote the part with Rourke in mind and he made the suggestions that resulted in the Motorcycle Boy resembling photographs of Albert Camus. The Motorcycle Boy even puffs cigarettes like the French existentialist writer.

Rumble Fish and *The Outsiders* were made back-to-back in Oklahoma during 1982. Both films were based on books about teenage angst by S. E. (Susie) Hinton. Both were directed in an unconventional style and were criticized when released in 1983 for overemphasizing emotions at the expense of narrative.

American film style generally stresses the art that conceals art. It's a macho thing inherited from the John Ford generation. If you shoot a scene through a mirror, do it so that the audience doesn't notice it. Use any device you like, but don't call attention to it. Otherwise, you stand in jeopardy of being 'mannered' or 'selfindulgent' or, worst of all, 'arty'. In American film-makers, selfconsciousness gets squashed quickly. Actors, too, fear this lash. A pause that lasts a millisecond longer than a critic is used to seeing on TV will call forth an impassioned jeremiad against 'the Method'. Repeating a look or a gesture can bring on the dread comment 'attitudinising'.

Thus a collective barrage of critical outrage greeted the first frames of *Rumble Fish*, in which clouds fast-forward across the sky. Coppola was telling a conventional story of misspent youth, but he was serving notice that he wouldn't tell it in a naturalistic manner.

Rusty James (Matt Dillon) is at a loose end because his revered older brother, the

Francis Coppola, director of Rumble Fish.

Matt Dillon and Mickey Rourke as reunited brothers Rusty James and Motorcycle Boy in Rumble Fish.

Motorcycle Boy, has left town after effecting a truce ending gang-fighting. Dillon manages to find a fight, though, and gets himself stabbed. Rourke arrives on his motorcycle, smiling and speaking softly, 'What is this, another glorious battle for the kingdom?'

The Motorcycle Boy is more myth than man. People say of him, 'He's a prince, you know. He's like royalty in exile.' They marvel, 'Isn't there anything he can't do?' Rusty James idolizes him and aches to be like him, but the Motorcycle Boy has one flaw. His father (Dennis Hopper) says the flaw is, 'Having the ability to do anything he wants to do and finding there's nothing he wants to do.'

In his tight T-shirts and clump-cut hair-style, Rourke plays this reluctant Pied Piper so softly that you hardly notice his little slip into madness. The Motorcycle Boy's pensive smiles get calmer and merrier. Chin in hand, face alight for some secret reason, he's less and less concerned about Rusty James' desire to be a delinquent and more and more wrapped up in a private dementia.

His madness is benign and self-sacrificial. He decides to take some Siamese fighting fish out of their tank in the pet shop and set them free in the river. He's shot dead in the act by the cop who's been hounding him all along. Rusty James then follows his brother's last wish – he frees himself by going off to California (though in Hinton's book, this trip to California was just another dead end for the boy).

The chilly reception accorded *Rumble Fish* was Rourke's first experience of the power of the Press to scoff. The Press loves to spot talent, put it on a pedestal and then knock it down. *California Magazine*, for instance, said, '*Rumble Fish* underlines Coppola's recent ten-

dency . . . to care more about camera angles than character.' As for Rourke, he 'could not be more selfconsciously wrong for the Hamlet-in-denim role he's taken on'.

Matt Dillon and Rourke in Rumble Fish.

The film Press had nothing in particular against Rourke; he was guilty by association with Coppola, who had recently bankrupted himself with the novel but costly *One from the Heart*. Coppola was paying off his creditors with his fees from his Hinton films, and many critics seemed to think he should knuckle under completely and make more ordinary-seeming films.

Rourke in Rumble Fish.

The courage to make such a film in the teeth of certain criticism is the quality Rourke most admires about Coppola. '*Diner* was nice and offended nobody, but *Rumble Fish* was a little experimental, innovative. I wanted to do it because at the time Coppola had his balls hanging over a fence and he still didn't try to do a "safe" movie.'

Rumble Fish.

Some actors are born to play younger brothers; others will always be the older one. Rourke's hard living has visibly marked his face. He was twenty-seven when he made *Rumble Fish*; and one of the characters in the film says, 'He looks so old sometimes, I forget he's twenty-one. He looks really old, like twenty-five.' Whatever age he plays, he has an air of having seen too much of the world and wishing to shield others' eyes from the sight. Twice in films he has played older brothers, just as he has done in his own life.

At the time Rourke was making *Rumble Fish*, his younger brother Joey was going through his first bout with cancer. He came close to death and was given the last rites twice. Rourke felt guilt that he hadn't been close to Joey in recent years and relief that he hadn't been taken away. So he tried to make up for lost time. He bought a house for Joey.

Rumble Fish has another haunting resonance with Rourke's offscreen life. In the film, Dennis Hopper plays a loving but ineffectual father to the Motorcycle Boy and Rusty James. The distance between father and sons and the thwarted love they all felt recalled to Rourke his own unresolved feelings towards his father.

After Rourke's reunion with his father in Schenectady, the two had begun rebuilding a relationship. They corresponded but didn't meet again. Then, in Oklahoma, working on *Rumble Fish*, 'They came to me on the set and told me my father was dying. So there was that whole thing going on with identity – who *was* my father? I was just starting to know him. We had just started writing. I was going to ask him to come visit. So I'd lost the opportunity to start to be buddies with him. It was too late. Too late for me and too late for the Motorcycle Boy too. It made me feel, you know, like there was no reason for me to be here any more, and I used that in the film. It was a painful time.' In early 1983, Rourke's father died.

SEVEN

The Pope of Greenwich Village was the film that was supposed to translate Rourke's undoubted audience appeal into box office dollars. To be sure, it was another offbeat character study, like all Rourke's films, but this script had a conventional genre hook — Mob boss goes after some small-time crooks. The plot worked for Walter Matthau in *Charley Varrick* – why not for Mickey Rourke and Eric Roberts?

Rourke knew this was his biggest chance yet: If any part was ever written for me, this is it, he thought. He prepared for the part like a boxer in training for a championship bout — although in this case the training involved getting out of shape, not in.

He gained two stone hanging out in restaurants in New York's Little Italy, just southeast of Greenwich Village, where the film was set. In a further search of the right look for his character, Charlie Moran, he spent $10,000 buying flashy Italian threads. He picked out the gorgeous sapphire pinky ring he slips on during the film's opening credits.

The touchiest part of the film's pre-production in 1983 was casting Rourke's co-star. Al Pacino was originally going to play the part of the feckless third cousin, Paulie. Pacino bowed out, though, after Rourke was cast as Charlie. Pacino thought Rourke was too young. The film's backers, MGM-UA, may have been disappointed, but not Rourke. He was elated to get the chance to work opposite Eric Roberts, 'the best actor I've ever worked with.'

The film's director, Stuart Rosenberg, said, 'Together, they're fascinating. You get the whole spectrum when you see the two of them together — in their physical attributes, emotions and approaches. They're sympathetic guys whom audiences side with immediately. They broadcast their drives, their fears, their vulnerabilities so cleverly that audiences forgive them no matter what they do.

'They are total opposites. Rourke is a street kid: tough, unpolished, but with an ingenuous quality I haven't seen since John Garfield stopped making movies. And as an actor, he plays it completely off the cuff – changes his lines from take to take, uses whatever's going on.'

Roberts is the opposite type of actor. He prepares meticulously and is always word-perfect from take one. But he put up with Rourke's sometimes unsettling way of working for the sake of the results. He says, 'Mickey would arrive on the set looking as if he'd just crawled out of bed and croak, "What scene are we shooting today?" I'd tell him, and he'd wander away. But he's great – the most naturalistic actor I've ever worked with. It didn't bother me at all.'

Rourke returned the compliment: 'Eric was so giving. He was *there*. We worked off each other so well, and there was a lot of love there – which is what the movie's all about. It's a love story: Charlie would rather be with Paulie than the girl.'

The two actors worked so well together, despite their differing styles, that they spoiled the film. That is, they took it out of the gangster genre altogether. Any chance it might have had to appeal to the shoot-'em-up audience was gone when Rourke and Roberts worked so close to the horns that only aficionados of fine acting appreciated their efforts.

Perhaps the audience misconstrued Eric Roberts' out-on-a-limb performance as a mannered actor's ego trip. Perhaps they couldn't understand the passivity of Rourke's character. Perhaps they wanted Rourke gri-

SCENE
IG

TAKE
4

PROD·POPE OF GREENWICH VILL.

IR. S. ROSENBERG

J. BAILEY

DATE
10·21·8

In The Pope of Greenwich Village *Rourke played a young man who loved the finer things in life but loved his messed-up cousin (Eric Roberts) more.*

mier. From the first frames of the film, Rourke is putting on a new persona, along with his $80 powder-blue shirt with monogrammed cuffs and his meticulously positioned tie-clip. Instead of the devil-may-care tearaway, this character, Charlie Moran, is controlled, cautious and very concerned about making the right impression.

Half-Irish, half-Italian, Charlie is a head-waiter at an Italian restaurant where his buddy and distant relative Paulie, works as a waiter. When they lose their jobs because Paulie cheats the owner out of half his cheques, it's no problem. Paulie engineers a score. They steal $150,000. Only after the heist does Charlie learn they were stealing from Bed Bug (Burt Young), the hoodlum whom Rourke calls the Pope of Greenwich Village. Bed Bug carves Paulie's thumb off, and worse seems on the horizon for Charlie. But in an ending considerably happier than that of Vincent Patrick's 1979 book, Paulie serves Bed Bug lye in his espresso. Charlie and Paulie walk off down the street to the sound of Sinatra singing 'Summer Wind'.

Charlie is continually telling Paulie about the errors of his ways, and he always ends up smiling indulgently at him. In contrast, Charlie forgives his girlfriend (Daryl Hannah) nothing. In his life, she's a distraction and she knows it. Rarely in a movie has a woman hit a man as often as Hannah hits Rourke in *The Pope of Greenwich Village*. Once she even wears a boxing glove when she clouts him.

Eric Roberts and Mickey Rourke in The Pope of Greenwich Village.

Rourke and Daryl Hannah in The Pope of Greenwich Village.

Before she leaves him, she slaps him around and chews him out: 'You just miss. You just miss. Another fucking inch, you know, and you could be someone special. But you're all caught up in your tribal loyalty and your neighbourhood and Paulie.' She slaps his face, and he says, 'Hit me again and see if I change.' Rourke gets a great exit: he adjusts his black leather jacket, puts on some shades, gives her his sweetest smile and goes down some stairs while she calls vainly after him.

It's a typically intense scene from a film with too many good scenes for its own good. Time after time, the actors transmit the emotional weight of an event before the audience understands what the event itself actually was. When Paulie's thumb is cut off, you know something bad is happening but you don't know what it was until later. You don't know Charlie and his girl have split for good until later, when he finds out she's taken his money. You don't know just how distasteful Bed Bug found his coffee until Paulie explains later why the man ran through a plate glass door. Maybe the audience likes its caper movies more transparent.

The Pope of Greenwich Village.

Reviewers generally declined to support the aspirations of the film-makers. 'Not so much a story as a collection of character studies,' said TV critic and film historian Leonard Maltin. 'It's a moderately entertaining bad movie,' wrote Pauline Kael dismissively – though she did give Rourke's dimples a rave: 'He has a confidential, flirty softness in his voice and an angelic, secret smile; his lips dimple up at the corners – he seems to be smiling in his head.'

When *The Pope of Greenwich Village* failed at the box office, Rourke was taken by surprise. He'd been so pleased with his work that he'd assumed the rest of the world would be too. He made the same mistake later on *Year of the Dragon*. Together, the two experiences contributed much to his present embitterment.

Before the film came out, Rourke couldn't say enough good things about it and its director. 'Francis [Coppola] is a god. He can do anything, and Stuart's the same way. Stuart Rosenberg is a genius. I want to do ten movies with him. I knew it would be hard to work on another film, because I've never liked anything as much as *The Pope of Greenwich Village*.'

He had to go to the extreme of cutting his hair short and dyeing it orange to shake off his Charlie Moran persona. He said, 'I feel that I'm a very lucky man. A lot of the anger I used to walk around with is gone now. I can channel it constructively, which makes it a lot easier for the people in my life: my wife and Sandra [Seacat] and Stuart.'

Euphoric though Rourke had been before *Pope* was released, he was dismissive afterwards. He decried his lack of control over the finished product, and there was no more talk of collaborations with Stuart Rosenberg.

'The movie has . . . problems. There are things about the movie that I like and things I have a lot of trouble with. Things didn't go totally like they should have. I thought there was something weird in the editing. I didn't understand the cuts.' In the end, the best he could say about the film was that it was 'as good as possible under the circumstances'.

Wearily, he agreed with Pauline Kael's diagnosis that the part wasn't much of a stretch for him. 'Charlie is who I would have been if I had taken a wrong turn.' 'I agree that it wasn't much of a stretch. But right now I only get paid for playing roles that are very close to myself. After *Body Heat* they were offering me all psycho roles. Nobody was offering me any great scripts before *The Pope of Greenwich Village*.'

EIGHT

'Heat' is a curious media concept describing qualities that are largely imaginary. Fame, talent, timing, looks, luck – all have something to do with heat. A star has heat at the point in his career when a large enough percentage of the entertainment industry think that a large enough percentage of the rest of the world is at a peak of interest in the star. In 1984, Rourke had heat.

He seemed to be the one actor under thirty who could back up his neo-beat poses with the ability to play characters. He looked young, but he also looked prematurely grown-up. He looked tough, yet nobody played tenderness better. Men and women seemed to respond equally to him. He could draw adults without going over the kids' heads. He seemed to be a Richard Gere with depth.

Despite the disappointment over *The Pope of Greenwich Village*, Hollywood felt sure that Rourke had heat. Projects became financeable on his name, and his price rose to the million-dollar range.

At this point of maximum seductiveness, Hollywood was failing to tempt its new blue-eyed boy into grabbing the brass ring. Two projects that absolutely exuded heat failed to secure his signature because he thought the scripts were inadequate.

A biopic about rock and roll pioneer Jerry Lee Lewis might have been made several times between 1983 and 1986 for ABC Theatrical Films or PolyGram Pictures. Rourke even learned to play 'Whole Lotta Shakin'' on the piano for the film. But the scripts that were written seemed too tame and TV-ish, and the project languished.

Legs, William Kennedy's novel based on the life of thirties' gangster Jack 'Legs' Diamond, was going to be one of the ten films Rourke hoped to do with director Stuart Rosenberg after *The Pope of Greenwich Village*. Kennedy's first draft script failed to attract studio interest, and *Pope* producer Gene Kirkwood had to drop the project.

Kirkwood had kept Rourke sweet by helping him out with a long-cherished notion – to direct himself in his own script about a boxer, *Home Boy*. The story would be based on a young boxer Rourke knew in Miami named Johnny Walker, who grew up to make crime his business instead of acting. His example helped deter Rourke from further involvement in risky business in Miami. Rourke strongly identifies with Walker and his struggle: where Rourke got involved with Hollywood, his hero in *Home Boy* gets involved with the Mob. The character in the script has a tough childhood, and the scars still show, as they do on Rourke.

Kirkwood handed Rourke $75,000 to take a film crew out to New Jersey on two weekends. At the time he was shooting *9½ Weeks* during the week. The venture was a disaster. Rourke knew little about the technicalities of handling a camera, and most of the footage he shot was not only unusable but unviewable.

But Rourke remained no less committed to his *Home Boy* script. Everybody he met heard him talk about it, and it was finally scheduled to go into production in November, 1987, in Atlantic City, New Jersey.

Home Boy and the other near-misses of that period were at least definite maybes. Other projects travelling the rumour circuit at the time of Rourke's maximum heat included a bank-robber buddy picture with Matt Dillon, a biopic about famed baseball player Ty Cobb, a film based on a novel by Alby Baker called *Stolen Sweets*, and a new treatment of

Mickey Rourke and Kim Basinger as the violent lovers in Adrian Lyne's 9½ Weeks.

the Wyatt Earp–Doc Holliday relationship (Rourke would have played the Burt Lancaster role, Eric Roberts would have played Kirk Douglas).

The film Rourke chose to do at the height of the rush to procure his services was *9½ Weeks*. Its failure when it finally limped onto the screen nearly two years after it was made is symptomatic of what's wrong with the American film business in the eighties. This flop is one answer to the question of why Rourke is not the Brando of his era, and why no one can be that kind of star now. *9½ Weeks* was damaged in pre-production, crippled in shooting, amputated in editing and murdered at the box office because its makers underestimated the audience, fearing their anger more than their indifference.

What might have been a milestone was blanded down into a routine movie. By the time it came out in February 1986, a year and a half after it was made, even Rourke didn't care any more. Instead of causing a scandal, like *Last Tango in Paris*, the film drew bored comments like *Variety*'s: *9½ Weeks* is a steer, not the bull it surely wanted to be.'

The film was based on a disturbing erotic tragedy written by the pseudonymous 'Elizabeth McNeill' (later identified as Ingeborg Day). The book, published in 1979 and entitled *Nine and a Half Weeks: A Memoir of a Love Affair*, was billed as a true story, and it had 'unfilmable' written all over it – and unfilmable it turned out to be, at least in America.

John (Rourke) is a stockbroker and Eliza-

Rourke and Basinger.

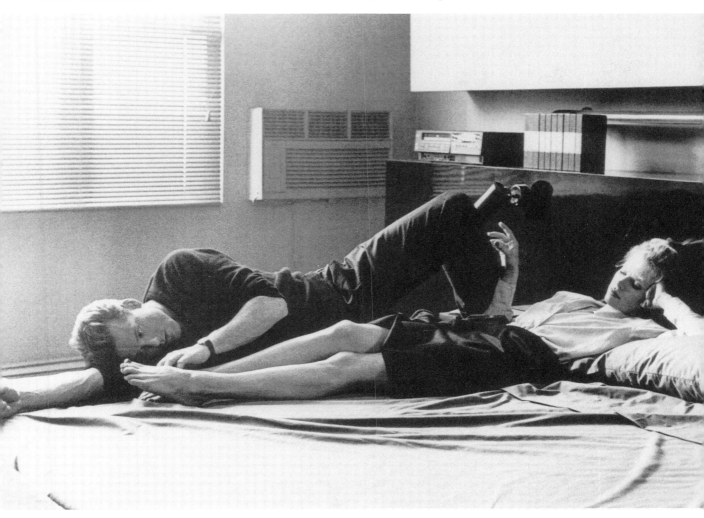

41

beth (Kim Basinger) works in an art gallery. They meet in a Chinese takeaway. He smiles, she looks disturbed. Another day, she's shopping in an outdoor market, and he's watching her, smiling. He keeps on smiling and when they finally exchange words, her first are, 'Every time I see you, you're smiling at me.'

Later, he tries to seduce her on a houseboat but she turns cold. Still later, he strands her high on a ferris wheel and she beats him in anger with a bunch of balloons. Soon, though, he is asking, 'Take off your dress,' and she is complying. And she is letting him blindfold her. He takes some ice and drips it on her and rubs it on her, and when he gets to her bellybutton the film cuts abruptly to Elizabeth's art gallery.

But something has happened, for the next time they're together, he's moved on to dripping raw egg over her. The time after that, he's throwing her on a table and ripping her clothes. All the time, she's telling her girlfriends, 'I can't figure this guy out,' but she can't stop seeing him.

The sexual teasing gets thicker and odder. He outfits her in a tuxedo and moustache and takes her to dinner. On the street afterwards, fag-baiters assault them, but she recovers a fallen switchblade and sticks one of the bad guys in the bottom. John and Elizabeth, turned on by the violence, make scrappy love on a stairwell under a dripping drainspout.

Gradually, though, what started as dominant-submissive becomes sado-masochism. John forces Elizabeth to accept the caresses of a prostitute, and she runs out to a peep show where she embraces the nearest voyeur. After this, Elizabeth knows she's in too deep. She walks out of John's apartment. To the closed door, John says, 'I love you, would you please come back by the time I count to fifty.' But she doesn't.

'When I first read the 9½ Weeks script, I felt it was truly something out of the ordinary in that it was from the woman's point of view. And I thought this kind of manipulation, this emotional detachment, is very close to what's going on with a lot of people in everyday life, but no one has really ever told the story this way before.'

9½ Weeks.

43

The script also offered Rourke a chance to play a different 'look' – a character with a white-collar job. 'They always want to throw me out onto the streets,' he said, referring to the working-class roles he had been offered up to then. 'They're not going to be able to keep doing it.' John had come up from the streets, Rourke theorized, but had found the key to middle-class respectability. 'He has learned that life is all a hustle, and he's turned this to his own advantage, and he's made the right turn.'

As he had with *The Pope of Greenwich Village*, Rourke insisted on buying his own wardrobe. He spent $12,000 on suits to wear in the film, but this time the director put him into costumes the art department preferred. Rourke did a little research on Wall Street, but it was so boring he stopped and decided to make the character his own kind of Wall Street guy. Because verisimilitude in bed would be more important than in the brokerage house, Rourke trained systematically for three months. He ran six miles a day and trimmed down to a full-frontal eleven stone. He kept up his training during pre-production even as the script was being revised to require less skin.

Why? Why change a script that reminded the film's bankable star of Harold Pinter? 'They just never shot the original script that I was fond of. The finished product wasn't what I thought it would be when I started. But that's nobody's fault. That's what happens when they want to shut you down four days before you're supposed to start,' Rourke said.

He added, 'The director wanted to make it more commercial. I had no say in the matter. Just like I had no say in *The Pope of Greenwich Village*. There are things you don't have control over. I signed up to do the script one way, and now I've got to do it another way.'

9½ Weeks was originally a Tri-Star production for director Sydney Pollack. But Pollack decided he preferred to do a softer love story, *Out of Africa*, instead. Adrian Lyne was hired to direct, but barely a week before shooting was to begin, Tri-Star dropped the project. The company that held the foreign rights, Producers Sales Organization, then took over the production and pre-sold it to MGM for US distribution. This tangled history helped ensure the subsequent post-production disputes and the eventual two-version release. The film seen in Europe included footage and scenes that were excised in America.

When he signed for the film, Rourke wasn't yet able to negotiate cast approval, a perk that more established stars can demand. Kim Basinger wasn't his first choice for Elizabeth, and after she was hired she declined to do certain scenes. The director, Lyne, was torn between attempting a *Last Tango in Manhattan* and a more conventional love story. Rourke argued in favour of going all the way with it, but everyone else involved in the film preferred to err on the side of caution. The result was a mishmash that went from the editing room to the video shops in America, with virtually no theatrical release in between.

NINE

Many actors seek solitude to commune with their muse. Rourke prefers the company of a few well-chosen males. He creates environments where men can hang out together. That's why he bought an Airstream trailer similar to the one he'd seen Coppola use as his headquarters on *Rumble Fish*. His Fish, as he calls the long, streamlined silver caravan, is his travelling HQ.

While Rourke and Debra Feuer were still together, they were apart even more than their work required. Rourke maintained his suite at the Mayflower in New York, complete with weight machines and a sauna. (He no longer keeps the expensive Mayflower penthouse.)

When he was in Los Angeles, he spent as much time as he could in his 'office' in a scruffy area of Beverly Hills. He inhabited the place until all hours, often sleeping over instead of going home to the house he and Feuer were renting. As long as Rourke had his pals around him, he was happy.

One August afternoon in 1985 was typical. It was the time in the life-cycle of a film when it's all over but the shouting. The final cut is locked in, the labs are busy striking hundreds of prints, the ads are already popping up on TV, and the actors are making nice with the Press.

Whatever the demons that he called up to play the hyper Captain Stanley White in the film he'd just finished, *Year of the Dragon*, they were at bay as he sat in his Beverly Hills office discussing the film just before its release.

This 'office', as Rourke called it, was a small suite of rooms that you'd be more likely to find in the back of a New York pool hall than on Maple Street in a residential area of Beverly Hills. The only concession to the idea of 'office' was a big desk that Rourke used as his base while roaming around the uncarpeted premises and directing the activities of his retainers. The dim lighting and the drawn blinds weren't conducive to office work and there was a distinct lack of office machines. This was Rourke's office the way a grease pit is a racing driver's office.

It was Rourke's place to go for behaving like a regular guy. When he didn't want to deal with the public, when he didn't want anything to do with his wife, when he wanted to meet someone on his own territory, he could go to the office and hang out.

Rourke ran his hand through his uncombed hair and fingered his stubbly chin as he talked quietly and amiably, in his carefully unrefined way, about his life outside films. 'Sometimes, when I get upset if they won't given certain movies the go-ahead, I say to myself, "I don't really care about acting. I'll go do something else." I fall back on that. There are those times when I can just put acting out of my mind. I could just hang out, you know. I like hanging out with the guys. We do stuff.'

In his office this afternoon were his trainer ('Eddie, my trainer — we run together') and a man named Tony Lip. Rourke refers to him fondly as 'my guy, Tony Lip'. Lip played a small part in *Year of the Dragon* after spending much of his adult life working at the Copacabana night club in New York.

Rourke has been known as a soft touch for helping aspiring actors. He says, 'I won't do that any more,' and mimes spitting on the floor to seal his intention. Then he smiles and contradicts himself.

Mickey Rourke in Year of the Dragon.

9½ Weeks.

'I will. I still do. In New York I live at the Mayflower Hotel. For four years the waiter bringing me my orange juice was Joey Chin. I saw that Joey was a stand-up kid – a real gentleman, yet you didn't mess with him.

'I like taking a guy who's really raw and working with him. Joey went in and read for a little part in *Year of the Dragon* and beat out six or seven other guys.' Chin's part, as the villain's chief triggerman, has few lines but many gunshots.

'I helped a few actors out. Three or four guys who are in the movies now who I won't name. I got them some parts, and then they got all neurotic. They got like babies.' One of the rising generation towards whom he used to act as godfather was Sean Penn. Now, without naming names, Rourke likes to contrast his exemplary public conduct with that of some other actors who have indeed been naughty: 'You don't see me punching out photographers.'

As for godfathering young actors, he says, 'I'd rather help out guys who aren't actors who really tear into the work because it's something

48

Above: Rourke with Linda Hamilton in the TV film *Rape and Marriage: The Rideout Case*

Below and above right: Rourke as Robert 'Boogie' Sheftell in *Diner*

Below and following page: Rourke in Nic Roeg's *Eureka*

With Ariane (Tracy Tzu) in *Year of the Dragon*

Rourke played Charlie Moran in *The Pope of Greenwich Village*

Above: with Eric Roberts, 'the best actor I've ever worked with', in *The Pope of Greenwich Village*

Below: As Stanley White in Michael Cimino's *Year of the Dragon*

better to do than just hanging out. If they can get some money out of it, hey, why not?'

Rourke enjoys being a mentor because he had a mentor. 'I had it done for me by Sandra Seacat, my acting teacher. Lots of times when I wasn't working she used to give me kids who weren't ready to be in her class, a dozen or so. I enjoyed laying on them what she'd taught me, knowing that out of the dozen or so there would be one or two who would take it and run.'

Rourke's preference for male companionship was a constant source of friction with his wife. Rourke and Feuer met soon after he landed in Los Angeles and married the following year when he was preparing to make *Diner*. She is an actress whose best part to date has been as the villain's girlfriend in *To Live and Die in LA* in 1985. It was Rourke's first adult relationship with a woman his own age. Previously, the women he'd stuck with for more than one night were older.

As Rourke moved quickly from being a promising nobody to being a million-dollar star, he indulged himself like a kid in a toy store. He bought a fleet of half a dozen expensive cars and a Harley-Davidson motorcycle. He also bought a house for Feuer – not for the two of them, but for her. For himself he bought his Airstream trailer and the lease on a penthouse suite in the Mayflower.

Rourke's and Feuer's relationship was one of near-continuous separation. 'I had a thing with my wife about the hotels that had come to a crossroads. I had to make a decision and think about what my priorities were. Besides, I get self-destructive in New York. Whatever schedule I try to put together, I can't seem to stick to it. I get too – well, I have too much fun.'

During 1984 Rourke was seen everywhere with actress Lauren Hutton. They went out together, they gave interviews together, they even crashed one of Rourke's Mercedes together. Feuer was at home, deeply into meditation (Rourke has even claimed he has seen her levitate).

Rourke and Feuer were further apart than ever after Rourke made *9½ Weeks* in 1984. 'My wife was very angry that I was making this movie. I wasn't sensitive to her needs. I isolated myself from her for three or four months, and I guess without realizing it I was getting into character in a very selfish way.' Eventually, without any great change in his habits, Rourke had to admit that he and Feuer weren't together any more. He called their separation a period of adjustment and said they would always be friends.

The distance between them was apparent on that summer day in 1985 in his office, when the phone on Rourke's desk rang. It was 'my old lady', Rourke said. Feuer overheard him and objected to the term. This made Rourke smile and hold the phone a foot away from his ear.

'She's at it again,' he said *sotto voce*, smiling. He turned his attention back to the phone and whispered sweet nothings for a while. Later he said, 'My wife tried to domesticate me. Then she gave up. I'm the kind of guy who won't go to sleep till my eyes shut by themselves. I'm afraid I'm going to miss something. I don't even like to go out till midnight.

'She'd like to go out earlier and she says to me, "I'd like a little romance in my life," and I say, "Debra, I live with you." But she's great. We're complete opposites. We have separate interests. She's a horsewoman, for instance. I tried to get involved in that – for a while. There's give and take. We've been married six years, and it works. As difficult as things can be, we're learning to be supportive of each other. One thing I know, I'll always be married to her.'

TEN

Rourke boasts that he has had a life-long problem with authority figures. He rebelled against his stepfather, and he's rebelled ever since against anyone who arrogated power over him. And yet he is known as 'a director's actor', eager to place himself in the hands of a master he trusts. Whatever the psychologists would make of that, the fact is that Rourke has developed fierce loyalties to particular directors. No matter how sloppy the soup their artistic choices have landed Rourke in, he has maintained his attachment to Francis Coppola, Alan Parker and Michael Cimino.

All three directors have a gutstring-grabbing style that often seems too intense for those who feel that life should be depicted as more manageable. In a literal-minded age, these directors use oblique strokes. Formalist rather than didactic, they make movies some decry as amoral. The effect they're aiming for has little to do with what can be synopsized. Story values can take second place to characterization. Impact sometimes supercedes logic. Rourke, who prides himself in starting life anew every day, loves to work for directors who go for broke in every scene.

Rourke had seen Michael Cimino striving for perfection on *Heaven's Gate* in 1979. Cimino sacrificed everything to his vision – including Rourke's part – but Rourke knew he wanted to be involved in this kind of all-stops-out film-making. Even after the non-release of the film and the collapse of the company that backed him, United Artists, Cimino's talent continued to attract producers. Cimino nearly agreed to direct *The Pope of Greenwich Village*, but he wanted too much time to re-orient the script. Instead, Cimino signed to make another gangster film about a nearby area of Manhattan, Chinatown.

'I don't think I would have did *Year of the Dragon* if the script had been sent to me by someone other than Michael Cimino, or someone of his calibre – which there aren't too many of,' Rourke said. 'There's what's on the page, and some directors will give you that, and other directors will give you that and more. Michael Cimino is that kind of director.

'It wasn't like I was sitting around dying to play a cop. It was the elements. You give and you take a little bit. If some of the elements work out, it might be worthwhile to do it. There are some roles where, maybe if some elements aren't right, you're so in tune with the character that you do it anyway.'

Rourke described working with Cimino as one long honeymoon. He declared, 'As long as I was working with Michael, I'd play a monkey, I don't care. Whatever anyone holds against him because of *Heaven's Gate* should be forgiven.' In contrast to his overspending on *Heaven's Gate*, Cimino underspent his budget on the $20-million *Year of the Dragon* and finished the four-location shoot three days ahead of schedule. Rourke says, 'Everyone on this picture knew not to start making any of the wrong kind of noise. Nearly every scene was done in four takes or less.'

Cimino's film begins and ends with gunshots, and there are plenty in between. Captain Stanley White takes over the Chinatown precinct just as smooth young businessman Joey Tai (John Lone) is moving to take over the area's dope-dealing tong. 'There's a new marshall in town,' White announces, and many murders follow.

White is the kind of cop who 'moves through this department like a piece of heavy machinery.' At home, he can't quarrel when his wife calls him arrogant and self-centred. So

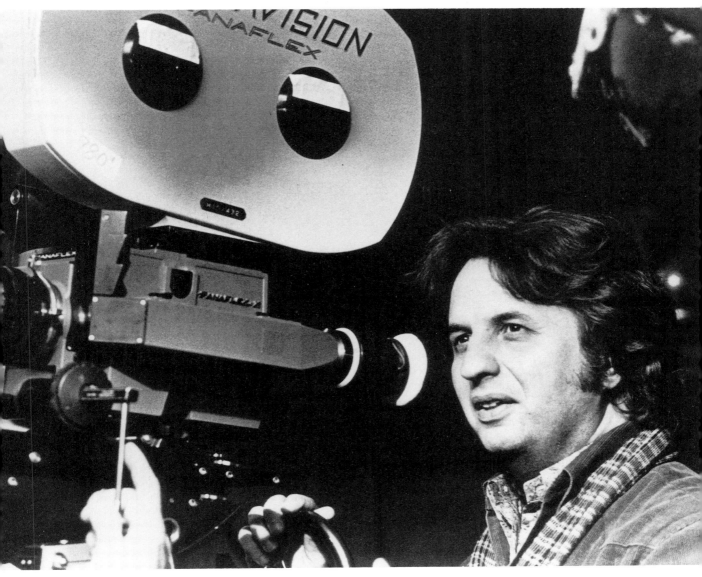

Michael Cimino, director of Year of the Dragon.

he shouts at his superiors and takes up with another woman. This is Tracy Tzu (Ariane Koizumi), a TV reporter. White and Tzu are attracted to one another but find themselves trading insults in Tzu's white-on-white apartment most of the time.

White pursues Joey Tai relentlessly, saying, 'Fuck their civil rights.' He tells the Police Commissioner, 'This is Vietnam all over again. Nobody wants to win this thing—flat-out win.' Tai's thugs kill White's wife. Then they rape Tzu. 'He went too far this time,' vows White. 'You care too much,' his boss accuses. 'How can anybody care too much?' White asks.

Before and since, Rourke has tended to play characters on the run from the police. To play a cop in *Year of the Dragon*, especially a true-blue 100 per cent law-and-order cop, Rourke said, 'They had to break a lot of stuff down with me. Most of it was physical. This cop didn't jitterbug, he walked straight. If someone did something wrong, this cop is on the side of right in two seconds.'

For most of his career, Rourke has played guys you had to love, no matter how much hell they raised. This time, Rourke was hard to love. Pursuing the ruthless Chinatown crime lord, Rourke as Stanley White shouted and gritted his teeth. This cop, so unlike the soft-voiced characters Rourke played before, had no time to smile.

'Michael wanted a certain pace to it. At the first rehearsal, he told me, "You're on the Force fifteen years. You're a captain. If you speak in the voice that people have normally heard you speak in, you won't project authority and command their awe. If you sound like Motorcycle Boy, nobody will pay attention." Michael whipped that on me. At first I was uncomfortable with it. Then I realized it was my first choice too.'

Throughout, Rourke willingly acceded to Cimino. 'Usually I know what I want to do with a character and the director leaves me alone, but Michael only let me do that to a degree. Michael wouldn't let me pick my wardrobe. He gave me the voice. He's the ultimate actor's director. The choices he makes – he knows exactly what he wants. He prepares a lot. He knows the time of day in every scene. We shot a lot out of continuity, but he knew where every piece fitted. Michael makes it easy on an actor.'

Rourke does recall making one decision about the character on his own: dyeing his hair grey. 'In the book the guy is fifty-four years old. I put his outfit on, his jacket and stuff. Something was incomplete. I knew it was age. I didn't want to go in for wrinkles. It had to be something else. The guy was a Vietnam veteran. His whole life had involved seeing death. I wanted that to be reflected physically, so you could see how he had been drained. I figured he had prematurely faced death, so I made him prematurely old, prematurely grey.'

Rather than read the 1981 novel by Robert Daley from which the film is taken, Rourke based his character on a real homicide detective, Stanley White of the Los Angeles County Sheriff's Department. 'I went out on thirty-two homicide calls with White. In the movie I wear my hat the way he wears his hat. I walk like him. I shoot a gun his way.' In homage, the character in the film is called Stanley White instead of the name he had in the book, Arthur Powers.

The film's Stanley White differs from the real Stanley White in that the character gets personally involved in a case. Rourke says, 'I asked Stanley, "Doesn't it get personal?" He said no. In the film, it does get personal. He's unable to stop it.' The real Stanley White impressed Rourke with his detachment in the presence of death. While Rourke was preparing the film, a beeper call at an odd hour would mean another corpse the actor had to go and stare at while White walked around the crime scene unaffected.

Rourke learned the ropes of Chinatown in the company of another cop. 'It was Joe Fusano, a cop in the Fifth Precinct – Chinatown. I went undercover with him. I met some Chinese gang members. He didn't tell 'em who I was,' and Rourke certainly didn't either.

'I'm very pleased with the way everything turned out,' Rourke said. 'I don't think I could have given the performance without all the research I did. For realism, the movie is pretty much on the money.' However, there were some concessions to showbiz. The year of the dragon doesn't come around in the Chinese calendar until 1988. 1985 was actually the less-catchy year of the ox. Moreover, the premise of the film, that the Chinese challenge the Mafia for control of drug traffic, 'hasn't happened yet,' Rourke conceded.

In addition, there is a point in the movie where the script dictates a moment of softness. Rourke has mortally wounded Joey Tai but he doesn't finish him off. Instead he gives his gun to the fallen foe.

Rourke says, 'It was my hardest scene in the film to do. I asked myself, How can I justify not killing him? It was a moment where I had to believe in the character's action and make it something I'd do – handing a loaded gun to the guy who'd had my wife killed. The only way I could justify it was to think that for Stanley White things had gone so far, maybe he'd think the guy would put him out of his misery. If Stanley White couldn't live with his wife gone and the knowledge that he'd caused all that pain, then maybe it wouldn't be so bad to check out.' When the real Stanley White heard about that scene, Rourke reports, he said, 'I would have blown the fucker's head off.'

After the filming of *Year of the Dragon* finished, Rourke was euphoric and he decided to mark the moment permanently. He had noticed that on his left forearm, Stanley White has a tattoo of a scale of justice with a skull on the scale and the number 187 inside the skull.

Rourke and Ariane as a TV journalist who becomes involved with Rourke in Year of the Dragon.

Ariane in Year of the Dragon.

Year of the Dragon.

187 is the paragraph in the California penal code that says murder is illegal. On his right forearm White has a tattoo of a clown. So Rourke himself went to a tattoo parlour and put a souvenir of the movie on his left shoulder: a leopard's head with the Chinese ideogram for 'year of the dragon'.

A tattoo seems very Rourke. In *The Pope of Greenwich Village,*' he had one painted on his shoulder in the same spot. Also very Rourke is the parting gesture he was bestowing on visitors to his office in the weeks before *Dragon*'s release in August 1985. In a cupboard he had stockpiled a cache of *Year of the Dragon* promotional material. Nobody left Rourke's office in those days without a *Dragon* poster and a special souvenir, a black and yellow *Dragon* long-sleeved T-shirt with the slogan on the back, 'Cimino Is Back'. Rourke was like a child sharing his favourite toy.

Rourke was so happy with his collaboration with Cimino that he had no hesitation in predicting that *Year of the Dragon* would be a success. 'I was sure the picture would be a hit too, that everything would be redeemed. But this is a business where you got to be lucky.'

To a certain degree, Rourke's optimism about the film briefly lured him into thinking Hollywood's way: 'I've never before cared whether a film of mine would be a blockbuster. But right now I can't make any more pictures six people are going to see. Maybe later on I can do that again.'

Rourke had been prepared for the intemperate criticism Cimino would attract for daring to get on with his career. 'Cimino warned me that the reviews might be controversial. He said, "There's going to be backlashes on the movie," mainly at him.'

Nevertheless, the devastating reviews and the unanimity of the negative response shocked Rourke. 'The whole thing is a crashing waste, and not a little racist to boot. But if Hollywood wants to go under, drowning in Michael Cimino's torrential wet dreams may be as good a way as any,' wrote John Simon, typically, in the *National Review*.

The aftermath of *Year of the Dragon* soured Rourke on much of the American media. Previously amiable with the press, he turned hostile. He vowed never again to speak to representatives of certain powerful newspapers because their critics had belittled Cimino. Rourke wasn't upset at anything the critics said about himself; his personal reviews were favourable. His reponse was like a streetfighter: if you attack my friend, you attack me.

'Hey! If somebody would give me a piece of paper and say, "Just sign here and you work with Cimino for the next ten years," I would sign it in two seconds.'

Year of the Dragon.

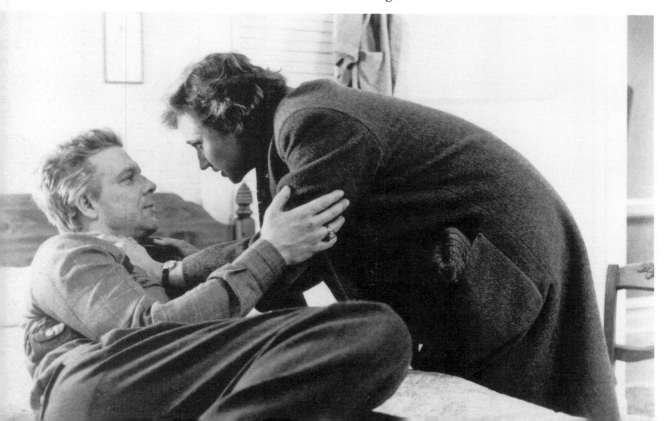

ELEVEN

After *Year of the Dragon* came out, Rourke stewed and seethed. All the combativeness of the Stanley White character found new expression as Rourke raged against the media.

In the spring of 1986 Rourke was in New York shooting *Angel Heart* for English director Alan Parker. One evening in April, as night fell over Seventh Avenue in Harlem, twenty progressively dingier blocks above Central Park, Rourke sat in the Fish with a gang of congenial spirits: his bodyguard, his driver, a Frenchman who hopes to direct Rourke in a future film and two or three others. The day's shoot had been in one of the neighbourhood's

Rourke with Alan Parker, director of Angel Heart.

many storefront churches, and everyone was ready to go downtown and party, except Rourke, who still had a few things to get off his chest.

'Stanley White is still inside me, and it's been a year and a half. When I put a coat on, the way I approach a door, I have to stop myself from doing it the way he would. Stanley White – may he rest in peace.'

But Rourke can't let Stanley White rest in peace. He's off on his favourite tangent: 'People don't want to know the truth. They're the scum of the earth, the critics who destroyed that picture. May they burn in hell, and you can put that down. The movie represented a certain type of passion, a sense of truth and honesty that intimidates people. They don't

Mickey Rourke in Angel Heart.

want to be reminded that those qualities exist. Cimino may be excessive. Look, if Reagan didn't lay the bombs on 'em [Libya] . . .'

Rourke pulls back from that particular brink and finds a way to end his tirade with a smile: 'I'm appreciated over in Europe. The writers and the young kids seem to have some sort of insight. I don't need it over here; as long as I know it's out there somewhere, I'm all right. I'll go over there and take care of my business. They want to make *Back to the Future* over here. I'm going to France. I'll sit in a corner and sip my coffee and be happy.' He has no intention of actually doing that, at least for any length of time in the foreseeable future, but the thought brings the hoped-for smile.

The production of *Angel Heart* was a time of healing for Rourke. Like many of his films, it offered such a rewarding artistic experience that it almost made the by-now-inevitable critical drubbing and subsequent box office fizzle endurable. Again, Rourke had attached himself to a director with a strong vision on the

screen and a light touch with actors.

'Alan is very much in tune with where I have to go and how I have to work. Without making speeches, he makes everything clear. He doesn't tell you how to get there, he just opens the way for you to get there. He's loose with the actors, yet you know he's in control. It's the easiest way of working – the only way of working. There's no ego, no games. Next after Cimino, I hold Parker in the highest regard.'

Angel Heart, set in the early Eisenhower era, was a typically Parkerish sojourn in a genre many lesser talents have explored before: the Devil goes after a soul he's bought and paid for but hasn't yet gathered into his fold.

'The character, Harry Angel, seems to be a regular guy,' as Rourke describes him, 'a regular knockaround guy in Brooklyn. He likes the simple life, going for a beer, getting laid whenever he can. He minds his own business, not everyone else's. He just gets by. He's an 8-to-4 guy. He works, he reads the comics, he takes a walk. One thing, though, he has a little memory problem.

Angel Heart.

'The guy gets a call from someone who asks him to go find someone who turns out to be himself. Harry's looking for the guy, and the audience is picking up things before he does. The audience is part of his discovery.'

Harry Angel isn't one of the world's greatest private detectives. Thus, he's a little puzzled when a mysterious and obviously well-heeled client styling himself Louis Cyphre (Robert DeNiro) arranges a meeting and offers big money for the whereabouts of one Johnny Favorite.

Favorite was a popular singer who disappeared fifteen years earlier, after being drafted into the Army during World War II. One trail leads Harry to a mental hospital upstate, one to a Father Divine-like religioso in Harlem, a third to deepest New Orleans. All the while, bells keep ringing in Harry's memory. He keeps flashing on two images: the back of a man in Army uniform who never quite turns his face to be identified, and an ominous elevator mechanism.

In Louisiana, Harry meets Epiphany Proudfoot (Lisa Bonet), an habituee of the voodoo world of decapitated chickens and worse. He also pays a call on a dabbler in the occult (Charlotte Rampling), later found dead, her heart cut out of her chest. The higher the pile of corpses and the closer Harry gets to discovering the truth, the more Louis Cyphre (Lou Cyphre, Lucifer, geddit?) smiles and buffs his long, glistening fingernails.

Eventually Harry realizes he's not really Harry, he's none other than Johnny Favorite. Harry was an innocent soldier whom Favorite killed. Favorite took Harry's identity, seeking a way to renege on the deal by which the Devil had given him success. In the end, Cyphre wins and Harry/Johnny finds himself in that Satanic elevator, going down, down, down, all through the closing credits.

At one time, the property on which the film is based, William Hjortsberg's 1978 novel *Falling Angel*, was owned by Robert Redford. After seeing Rourke play this ambiguous hero, it is hard to imagine such a straight leading man in the role.

'Rourke doesn't fit the image of the conventional goody-goody hero,' says Alan

'That's one reason he's a private detective. He's always searching for something, he doesn't know what. It's like – are you a happy man? You know if you are or you aren't. Still, there's something gnawing inside everybody, not necessarily painful like you're a character in Chekhov, but it's there.

Rourke with Charlotte Rampling in Angel Heart.

60

Angel Heart.

Parker. 'There's a side of him that isn't — wholesome? I don't know the right word — which I find attractive. He's likeable without fitting the Hollywood cliché definition of the word.'

Rourke's job in *Angel Heart* was a difficult and possibly thankless one. Where a Redford would have insisted on looking smart and acting smart, Rourke wore a slovenly exterior and a perennially puzzled look. He had to win the audience's sympathy by very subtle means.

However, any subtlety attached to the making of *Angel Heart* was overridden when the film was ready for release. Shock! Horror! There was a love scene that America's ratings board thought was too effective. Rourke and Bonet are making love in a conventional pos-

ture and with a degree of flesh exposure no more extensive than countless titillating scenes in other movies — except Parker wasn't aiming strictly at arousal here. By intercutting shots of the actors on a bed with shots of blood seeping, dripping, flowing, eventually cascading through the room, he heightened the scene's impact to X-rating levels, according to the ratings board.

In the weeks before the film's release date, Parker negotiated with the censors, trimming the scene frame by frame to avoid the X-rating. That was necessary because in America the X has come to denote porno films. Many newspapers and TV stations will not accept ads for X-rated films.

Rourke was in Los Angeles filming *Barfly* during those fraught weeks in February and March 1987. Parker was a constant visitor to the *Barfly* set, closeted in the Fish with Rourke

Angel Heart.

between takes. Rourke agreed to appear with Parker during one of the director's appeals to the ratings board.

The Press loved this made-to-order controversy. It put *Angel Heart* in the headlines, but unfortunately it focused attention on the film's alleged salacity and obscured the filmmakers' overall intentions. The dominant tone of the reviews in America was amused disdain. Though some praised Rourke – *Newsweek* found 'new depths' in his acting – his performance was largely ignored in the rush to belittle Parker. Comments about the actor were generally limited to jokes about his costumes and lack of barbering.

'Stubbled eyesore Mickey Rourke, his wardrobe apparently stomped on by a flamenco dance troupe ...' said *USA Today*. 'You're likely to note that as 1955's Harry Angel, he sports the same two-day-old, male-

model stubble (and *Miami Vice* wardrobe) he used for his 1986 character in *9½ Weeks*,' said the *New York Times*.

Rourke attracts uncomprehending notices like these because 'the people on the periphery of the creative process,' as Parker calls the film Press, are looking for concrete things to write about. Rourke, however, likes to keep things vague. His acting style is subtly off-the-beat, unemphatic, full of out-of-nowhere moments.

Asked about his tendency to choose movies with challenging subjects, he shrugs, 'You can't please everyone. There's movies I'll make that the majority will want to see, but right now I'm not making movies for everyone to see. A studio wants to make movies for everyone to see. I'm not a studio, I'm an actor.'

In the Fish that spring night in Harlem, Rourke retained the edginess he needed to film scenes involving sights better left unseen. As filming had proceeded that day, he stalked unapproachably back and forth between the storefront church that served as the set and the Fish, which served as his refuge, until the moment seemed right to let down his guard a little.

You can't pin Rourke's characters down, and you can't pin him down in person, either. It's partly the evasiveness bred into him during his seven-in-a-room upbringing. He learned self-protection early, and he remains ready for a scrap at all times. He's quick to issue comments like, 'Some people are uptight about someone they can't mess with. You can't jerk me around. You can't mess with me.'

Film by film, Rourke has drifted into an adversarial position towards Hollywood and its ideas of how to run the film business. 'I never get sent scripts by the studios,' he says, a bit proudly. 'The studios aren't making movies like the ones I want to make, so things are working out fine for me because I'm not very caught up in the commercial aspect of making movies.

'Look who's running the studios. There's a different guy every week. The studios are into making money; I'm into making movies I believe in. When I started out, I had no great love of acting. I had to acquire it. Now that I got it, I'm using it.

'I make my career choices, but choices I can live with – otherwise I might as well check out. I'm my own boss, but you never hear about me punching people out. I come to work on time, I do my work, I collect my money, compromising where I have to, and I make my next choice. Simple.'

Rourke looks down the aisle of the Fish, where his cronies are sitting like crows on a phone wire, nodding their heads. They're like a gallery for Rourke to play to. He continues, 'This acting stuff, it's not what you think it is, or want it to be. It's a job. Sometimes you like it, sometimes not. Sometimes they love you, sometimes they hate you.

'I'll tell you: I can't do anything for the money. If I lose respect for the director a

Angel Heart.

64

quarter of the way through the picture, there's going to be trouble. So I've got to make sure I respect the project and know the reason I'm making it, and know that not everything I'm going to do will be liked. And I learned that the hard way.

'It's like old Harry Angel. I like Harry. He's like a golf ball. He goes up and down the course and doesn't know what hole he's going in. Selling out can happen in a lot of different ways. You make deals, not with the Devil, but within yourself, and you change. Like me. I'm now successful, and as a result things are happening that I don't like. You do sell your soul, in a way, and you have to live with that.

'It's no picnic. Everyone thinks it is. I was in a bar the other night. I was combing my hair in the mirror and this guy comes up behind me and says, "You make too much money." And I said, "Hey, if they give it to me, I'll take it."

'That guy, he was half right and half full of shit. I'll compromise when it's necessary. But I'm my own man. If I sign my name, I'll do what I said I'd do, but because it was my choice. When I do what they want me to do, I do it because I chose to put myself in that position. That's my compromise, and if people don't like that they can kiss my ass.'

Rourke looks around at his lieutenants, making sure they're still with him. 'Acting – it's not a free ride. I got a lot of people counting on me. It's a job, what I do. It's turned into that. I take my money to the bank and then I go on holiday. I'm just trying to save enough money to take all the boys here and get on the Silver Fish and drive off and never come back. Right, guys?'

TWELVE

Alienated from the Hollywood film system, Rourke next chose to work abroad, where he figured he was appreciated. What should he find in England in the autumn of 1986 when he was making *A Prayer for the Dying* but the long arm of Hollywood stretching out to grab his throat.

When rehearsals are going badly, actors in the theatre have a saying, 'It'll be all right on the night.' Film actors don't have an equivalent shibboleth, but they often have to enmesh themselves in the film-making machine before they know for sure what kind of cookie it's going to cut.

What happened to Rourke on *A Prayer for the Dying* was that he and the producer and the producer's backer all thought they were making different films. Rourke thought he was making a cautionary tale about a man of vio-

lence trying and failing to redeem himself. American distributor Samuel Goldwyn Jr thought he was making an action film about revenge. Producer Peter Snell thought he was making a film that Rourke could respect and Goldwyn could sell.

Prayer began as a 1975 paperback pot-boiler by Jack Higgins. Borrowing a device from Alfred Hitchcock's 1953 film *I Confess*, its plot turns on a killer's confession that a priest cannot divulge.

Rourke plays Martin Fallon, an assassin for the Irish Republican Army who burns out and abandons the struggle. He has lived by the gun, and now that he has put down the gun, he has nothing to live for. He is the one referred to

Mickey Rourke with Bob Hoskins in Prayer for the Dying.

in the title, the one who is dying.

In the East End of London, a mortician who is actually a gangland boss (Alan Bates) offers Fallon a ticket to America if he'll kill a man for him. A priest, Father Da Costa (Bob Hoskins), has witnessed the murder but cannot report it because Fallon has sought absolution in his confessional.

Rourke took the part, knowing that the brutality in the book was far beyond anything he wanted to portray. He had been talking about the project with producer Peter Snell for a year and a half, and the body count was a concern he stressed constantly. An initial script by writer/director Franc Roddam was put aside. Edmund Ward, an Irishman who had adapted Jack Higgins' earlier novel, *The Violent Enemy*, into a 1968 film, was enlisted to rewrite the script.

'This was a writer who knew the material from first hand,' Rourke said. 'My grandparents come from over there [County Cork], and I wasn't going to have some Hollywood asshole make *Rambo* out of the issue. I went to Belfast. I spent time with people from the IRA. I can't say who they are – I don't want the FBI on my ass.

'I learned about the problem, how the Catholic minority's civil rights get stomped on like the blacks in America, how little boys see their fathers and grandfathers unable to get work because of their religion. I saw the graveyards filled with guys who died at eighteen, twenty or twenty-two. I saw that I had the opportunity to make a movie that could say something positive and could explain why a guy turns to the IRA.'

Rourke wasn't totally pleased with the director, Mike Hodges, an Englishman experienced in action films. But his real problem during shooting was caused by friction with the film's American distributor, the Goldwyn Co. 'I took half my salary to do this picture,' Rourke said. 'I waited five months to start it. Hoskins and Bates got involved because I was in it.

'The producer kept telling me, "We'll make the movie any way you want to do it." He didn't mention Samuel Goldwyn. Then the first day of shooting I learn that Goldwyn is involved. On my name, Goldwyn is selling the picture off to other territories so he can get more money and power to continue to make mediocre, crappy movies.

'If I'd known Goldwyn was in on it, I'd have protected myself in my contract.' Lacking that protection, Rourke was vulnerable to 'suggestions' from Goldwyn in Hollywood. Goldwyn, intent on protecting his investment in the £6-million project, sent memos to the location. Rourke's performance was deemed 'lethargic'. His Irish accent seemed 'hard to understand'. The script should be 'toughened'.

To Rourke, these notes were so many stabs in the back. Mentions of his contractual obligations seemed to him to be threats to sue: 'Samuel Goldwyn was threatening to sue me every day because I wouldn't make a *Rambo* movie. He knew I wasn't Chuck Norris or Arnold Schwarzenegger, and yet he was "afraid of the direction you are heading in". He sent over a go-fer to change my lines, to tell me not to do the accent, to try to get me to kill more people.

'They wanted me to do a love scene with an actress who looked fifteen. I said, "Yes, if you cast someone older." They agreed, sitting in a room with me, but of course they didn't sign anything, and I didn't sign anything.

'In acting class there's no three-year course in how to deal with producers who inherit their position. Things get very political, and I treat it the way I would when I feel disrespect on the street. I fight back. I announced a press conference, and then they backed off.'

Depending on his degree of anger at Goldwyn at any given moment, Rourke either expresses mild support for the finished film or completely disavows it. In angry moments, he says, 'I'm ashamed I made it. But I'm not through with the issue. I'll make another Irish movie. I'll get across the point I want to make. I'm already looking into the rights to a certain person.'

Bobby Sands, who died in May 1981, leading a hunger strike in the Maze prison, is one figure in the history of the sectarian conflict whom Rourke often mentions, though he'll go no further in identifying the subject of his proposed second Irish project.

When Rourke came home from England after making *A Prayer for the Dying*, he went into an artistic tailspin. Never much of a sleeper, he knew needed sedatives prescribed

Prayer for the Dying.

Prayer for the Dying.

by a doctor to get any rest at all. 'I was so fucked up mentally and physically, I was terrified to go back to work. I thought I was going to flip out. But I was lucky. I ended up here.'

'Here' is inside the Fish in Los Angeles, making another film. *Barfly* was the perfect film to help Rourke rebound from depression. It's a light yet penetrating look at an artist working through his pain. For *Barfly*, Rourke again had the conditions he needs to enjoy his work: a character that forces him to take chances, a director who believes in Rourke's methods, and a production company that disappears.

It's a balmy midnight in the real Los Angeles, the one the natives know, the town for which Raymond Chandler coined the phrase 'mean streets'. Rourke's Fish is pulled up outside the seedy Bryson Hotel. The Bryson stands at the other end of Wilshire Boulevard from the Beverly Wilshire Hotel, where stars are more apt to be seen. The Bryson is where Rourke's character, Henry Chinasky, sleeps off his drinks and writes his stories.

Chinasky is a self-destructive writer whose principal alienation is from the system that might turn him into a 'successful' author. He prefers the company of his fellow barflies to the pretentious hangers-on who are drawn to literary success. The film could be subtitled *Portrait of the Artist as a Young Drunk*.

In his favourite bar, the Golden Horn, Chinasky can dissipate without pressure. He can brawl without consequences. He can love without commitment. In the bar, Chinasky meets Wanda Wilcox (Faye Dunaway), another lush who has seen better days but liked them less. To Chinasky, she 'looks like some kind of distressed goddess'. Their affair is quick to ignite and apt to fizzle. When she says she doesn't want to fall in love with him, he says, 'Don't worry. Nobody's ever loved me yet.'

Prayer for the Dying.

Chinasky is tracked down by Tully Sorenson (Alice Krige), the rich proprietor of a literary magazine that has been publishing Chinasky's stories. This glorified groupie wants to lionize Chinasky and lead him around on a leash to all the best salons. Chinasky wants no part of her. For a start, he'd have to dry out, and drinking is too much fun when it's not hell.

Chinasky once was a boxer and despite the abuse he pours down his gullet every waking moment he still can throw a punch. The night bartender at the Golden Horn, who fancies himself as a fighter, takes Chinasky out into the alley behind the bar. Once Chinasky wins, once Chinasky loses.

At the end Chinasky, having declared his independence from life, returns to the bar after scoring some cash from the magazine. He buys drinks all around and toasts the gang, 'To all my friends! To all my friends!' But the price of being the star of the bar is a third round with the bartender. Whichever way the fight goes,

Chinasky won't mind.

Aside from the boozing, *Barfly* could have been written as a veiled biography of Rourke, who has chosen an independent artistic path in a highly commercialized industry. Actually, the *Barfly* script is a fairly literal piece of autobiography by celebrated Meat School poet-novelist-survivor Charles Bukowski.

Bukowski is one of America's least celebrated authors, though in Germany and France he is revered. The film's existence is the result of French director Barbet Schroeder's obsessive nine-year pursuit of the author. Schroeder eventually convinced Bukowski, who had never written a film script before, to try the medium.

The script was published in 1979. Actor-director Dennis Hopper saw it several years later and brought it to the attention of Sean Penn, the actor and photographer-puncher.

Penn volunteered to star in the movie for no salary as long as Hopper were the director. Bukowski was happy with Penn but felt committed to Schroeder.

Several more years passed before Schroeder sold the idea to Cannon, the upstart company that has bankrolled some fairly adventurous films. What sold Cannon was not the script or the director but Rourke. Deeply unhappy with *A Prayer for the Dying*, Rourke accepted *Barfly* 'overnight', Schroeder says. 'So overnight that the next day I met with Menahem Golan of Cannon, who accepted in five minutes.'

Rourke says, 'When I first read the script, I thought it was a very dark piece. When we started to shoot it, I saw the humour.' To play Henry Chinasky, Rourke has gone deeper into disguise than he ever has before. If critics were offended by his two-day's growth in some recent films, the sight of Rourke's neglected near-beard in *Barfly* should send them scampering for their mother's skirts. The character's hair, an untended mess, resembles a buckskin fringe, and his wardrobe is direct from the dump. His knuckles are blackened by his opponents' unbrushed teeth. His lower jaw juts out from under a laughing grimace. You can practically see him stink.

Most offensive to the shrub-tending Aunt Sallies in the public prints will be Rourke's accent. Henry Chinasky sounds like he left his voice in a gutter. All his sentences fade away and die at the end. They start with a whoop and end with a whine. Chinasky's almost child-like locutions allow Rourke to put emotions on the soundtrack more nakedly than ever.

The accent and the look were last-minute choices. Typically, Rourke relied on the inspiration of the moment and then committed himself fully to that impulse. 'I committed to do the film five months before we started, but I was so fucked up after *A Prayer for the Dying* that I wouldn't even talk to Schroeder about the character until two days before we started shooting.'

When they finally talked, Schroeder brought Bukowski along. Rourke had never heard of Bukowski before the idea for the film was put to him, and he had never met the 66-year-old author until that day. 'As a man, Bukowski seemed genuine,' Rourke concluded, and on the spot he decided to borrow Bukowski's dying-fall manner of speaking.

'I made the choice to talk like him in about ten minutes. I never had any energy to research this part. So you can say I'm winging it. I decided that unless I went all the way with this character, I'd wind up being mediocre. I decided to make the guy real, not like he was in a Hollywood fucking commercial movie, not like it was directed by John Landis. I took a chance going all the way, not caring if I went too far.'

Part of what makes Rourke such a fascinating figure to those who can stand to stay on his wavelength is the feeling he gives that any minute he'll fall off the cliff. Virtually all of his characters have been men at the end of their tether, willing to lose everything for the sake of some fixed idea of themselves they can't put into words.

Of Henry Chinasky, Rourke says, 'He's a guy who has alienated himself from everything that stands for anything. He doesn't give a shit about pity, for himself or anybody else. He's not easy to love.

'He writes to shake off his dreams. He drinks to numb himself, but it's very hard for him to get drunk and achieve numbness. He doesn't want to be part of the human race any more. You strive and you struggle and you shit on people and they shit on you and what have you got left at the end? You're old. It isn't worth it.

'This character is very close to how I feel about my profession right now. It's an introspective exercise, in a way. *Barfly* came along at the right time to help me get my shit together and rejuvenate my feeling for my profession.'

As an actor, Rourke has always imposed impossible standards on himself. Working in an industry based on getting along and going along, Rourke has likewise demanded absolute freedom for artists and total commitment from their backers. These demands are hardly ever met in the real world, 'unless you're Woody Allen,' Rourke admits. Yet he keeps on behaving as if each new choice were the most important in his careet. Camus on a motorcycle?

As they say in Hollywood, sometimes the shark bites Rourke, sometimes Rourke bites the shark. As they say in Existentialism class, sometimes Rourke is the murderous Meursault in *L'Etranger*, sometimes he's the life-saving Dr Rieux in *The Plague*.

He says, 'I used to care so much about acting as a profession, as a thing to do in life. Now it seems that people settle for a level of mediocrity. They don't care for truthful acting. They prefer hype. They prefer reading about it in *People* magazine. Who knows, maybe I've been naive.

'I used to feel that acting was a pure thing: trying to master the Stanislavski technique, learning to reproduce life on a moment-to-moment basis. Now I don't think people care. Maybe I care too much.

'Now all it boils down to is a job. I'm fortunate to be a working actor. I'm not giving up, and I won't be bitter. Maybe it's taken a long time for me to see the world as it really is. There's always a price to pay. There's always a price to pay. You always think there's a pot of gold at the end of the rainbow, and you finally get there and it's a pot of boiling water with sharks moving around.'

But Rourke jumps in anyway. 'When the camera is running, when that red light is on, I always feel very good. Most actors, to me, have two left feet. I know what other guys can do, and I know what I can do. I can deliver. As long as I can, and as long as there are directors who've got a set of balls and will hire me, I'm okay.

'We'll see. In ten years, we'll know. Charles Bukowski says, "I always thought I'd be discovered after I was dead." That's the way it is for some.

'For me, as long as I get my paycheck and I can take care of my family and ride my Harley-Davidson, I'm all right.'

Mickey Rourke as Henry Chinasky in Bartly.

FILMOGRAPHY

FILMS:

1941 (1979), directed by Steven Spielberg, starring Dan Aykroyd, John Belushi, Robert Stack, Treat Williams.

Fade to Black (1980), directed by Vernon Zimmerman, starring Dennis Christopher.

Body Heat (1981), directed by Lawrence Kasdan, starring William Hurt and Kathleen Turner.

Eureka (1981), directed by Nicolas Roeg, starring Gene Hackman, Theresa Russell and Rutger Haver.

Diner (1982), directed by Barry Levinson, starring Mickey Rourke, Kevin Bacon, Steve Guttenberg, Daniel Stern.

Rumble Fish (1983), directed by Francis Coppola, starring Matt Dillon and Mickey Rourke.

The Pope of Greenwich Village (1984), directed by Stuart Rosenberg, starring Mickey Rourke and Eric Roberts.

Year of the Dragon (1985), directed by Michael Cimino, starring Mickey Rourke and John Lone.

9½ Weeks (1986), directed by Adrian Lyne, starring Mickey Rourke and Kim Basinger.

Angel Heart (1987), directed by Alan Parker, starring Mickey Rourke and Robert DeNiro.

Prayer for the Dying (1987), directed by Michael Hodges, starring Mickey Rourke, Alan Bates, Bob Hoskins.

Barfly (1987), directed by Barbet Schroeder, starring Mickey Rourke and Faye Dunaway.

TV MOVIES:

City in Fear (1980), starring David Janssen.

Act of Love (1980), starring Mickey Rourke and Ron Howard.

Rape and Marriage: The Rideout Case (1980), starring Mickey Rourke and Linda Hamilton.

PHOTO CREDITS

Photographs were supplied or are reproduced by kind permission of the following:

B.P.G. 18, 20

Canon Columbia Warner Distribution Ltd 58, 60, 62, 63, 65

Kobal Collection 11, 22, 28, 30, 36, 55, 57, 59, 61

National Film Archive 15, 23, 24, 26, 27, 29, 31, 34, 35, 37, 41, 48, 51, 52, 54, 56

Photo Graphics 12, 67, 69, 70, 71

P.S.A. Public Relations Ltd 40, 42, 44

Rex Features 9, 13, 47, 73

Ronald Grant Collection 26, 32

Tri-Star 10

COLOUR
1. Rex Features
2. *Rape and Marriage*: Lorimar
   Diner: UPI
3. *Diner*: UPI
   Eureka: UPI
4. *Eureka*: UPI
5. *Year of the Dragon*: Kobal Collection
6. *The Pope of Greenwich Village*: Ronald Grant Collection
7. *The Pope of Greenwich Village*: Ronald Grant Collection
   Year of the Dragon: Rex Features
8. Rex Features